Sainsbury's
WOODTURNING
PROJECTS for DINING

Sterling Publishing Co., Inc.   New York
Oak Tree Press Co., Ltd.   London & Sydney

Library of Congress Cataloging in Publication Data

Sainsbury, John A.
  Sainsbury's Woodturning projects for dining.
  Bibliography: p.
  Includes index.
  1. Turning. 2. Treenware. 3. Tableware.
I. Title. II. Title: Woodturning projects for dining.
TT201.S18   674'.88   80-54347
ISBN 0-8069-5436-1   AACR2
ISBN 0-8069-5437-X (lib. ed.)

Oak Tree ISBN 7061-2790-0

Copyright © 1981 by John Sainsbury
Published by Sterling Publishing Co., Inc.
Two Park Avenue, New York, N.Y. 10016
Distributed in Australia by Oak Tree Press Co., Ltd.
P.O. Box J34, Brickfield Hill, Sydney 2000, N.S.W.
Distributed in the United Kingdom by Oak Tree Press Ltd. U.K.
Available in Canada from Oak Tree Press Ltd.
% Canadian Manda Group, 215 Lakeshore Boulevard East
Toronto, Ontario M5A 3W9
Manufactured in the United States of America
All rights reserved

Contents

Introduction 4

LAYING THE TABLE
1 Candleholder 6
2 Bud Vase 11
3 Dinner Mats 15
4 Coasters 17
5 Napkin Rings 18

FIRST COURSE — STARTERS
6 Hors d'Oeuvre Dish 24
7 Grapefruit Dish

SECOND COURSE — SOUP
8 Soup Bowl 34
9 Bread Dish with Handle 37
10 Toast Rack 39
11 Pepper Mill 42
12 Salt and Pepper Shakers 44

THIRD COURSE — MAIN DISH
13 Dinner Plates and Side Plates 47
14 Side Salad Bowls 52
15 Goblet 59
16 Carafe 64
17 Salad Servers 68
18 Mustard Pot 72
19 Carving Board 74
20 Sauce-Bottle Holder with Lid 76
21 Salt Mill 81
22 Wine Bottle 89

FOURTH COURSE — DESSERT
23 Fruit Bowl 92
24 Fruit Dish 96

FIFTH COURSE — CHEESE & CRACKERS
25 Cheese Board 98
26 Cracker and Butter Dish 101
27 Butter Dish 105
28 Cracker Barrel 108

SIXTH COURSE — NUTS
29 Nut Bowl with Waste Rim 112
30 Nut Dish with Pick Container 117
31 Nut Bowl with Wheel Cracker 122

SEVENTH COURSE — COFFEE
32 Cups and Saucers 126
33 Sugar Bowl 133

EIGHTH COURSE — PETIT FOURS
34 Petit Fours Dish 136

FOR THE KITCHEN
35 Steak Tenderizer 140
36 Mortar and Pestle 142
37 Nutmeg Grinder 144
38 Coffee Grinder 149
39 Rolling Pin 157
40 Potato Masher 159

FOR BREAKFAST
41 Marmalade or Jam Pot Top 164
42 Egg Cups 168

APPENDICES 173

INDEX 189

Introduction

This book is designed as a book of projects to assist the woodturner with ideas. It is not a complete textbook of woodturning; techniques are dealt with as they arise in a project and not under a specific chapter heading. Methods suggested for holding the wood are those which I consider best for that particular job, but it is not intended that they shall be strictly adhered to or that a particular method is the only correct one. The woodturner may, in many cases, not have some of the equipment recommended, but there is a sufficient number and variety of methods to satisfy everyone.

As the woodturner gains in experience, so his knowledge of woods will become more extensive. He will, in time, be able to select the most suitable wood for a project, always keeping in mind the use to which the work will be put. This is particularly important where food is to be in contact with the wood. The woods used in the projects are those which I have found suitable. They may not be available to readers in some parts of the world, but satisfactory substitutes can be found almost everywhere.

Polishes must suit the particular purpose to which an article is to be put. There are many excellent polishes available, and the woodturner, over a period of time, will determine his favorite ones and probably use only a limited number.

Shaping—inside work (see "Appendix D, Using the Tools").

This craft can be one of the most enjoyable pastimes a person can have. Learn to cut wood properly, and aim to use less sandpaper, obtaining a good finish from the tool instead. You will save time in this way but, more importantly, your turnings will be crisp and unmarked.

LAYING THE TABLE

1 Candleholder

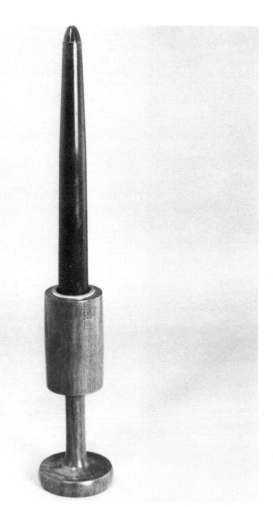

Fig. 1:1

Design Specification

A one-piece turning designed to hold a single candle **(Fig. 1:1)**.

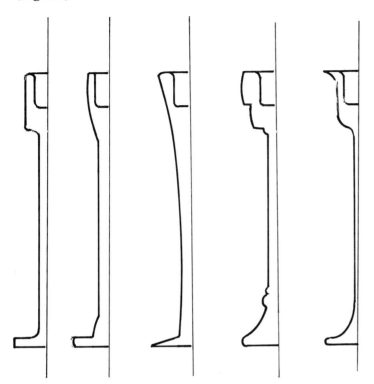

Wood

Use an attractive wood with long, straight grain to enable the stem to be turned thin.

Finish

A two-part acid catalyst finish or some other water-resistant type.

Attachment to the Lathe

Square the end of the wood and mount it on a screw chuck.

Lathe Speed

1400 rpm reduced to 800 rpm when boring.

Tools

¼-in. (6.3-mm) and 1-in (2.5-cm) spindle gouges
1-in (2.5-cm) skew chisel
Sawtooth machine bit or flat bit
Screw chuck
Tailstock drill chuck

Method

Spindle turning.

Turning the Candleholder

Screw the wood to the screw chuck, but first square one end. Rough down to round. Mark out with pencil and parting tool (**1:2**). Shape with the gouge (**1:3**). Square the end with the long corner of the skew chisel (**1:4**). Plane the stem with the ½-in (12.7-mm) skew chisel (**1:5-6**). Place a ½-in. (12.7-mm) sawtooth cutter in the tailstock drill chuck and carefully bore out the hole to receive the brass insert (**1.7**). Insert the brass cup (**1:8**) and fix with either glue or screw. Polish.

Fig. 1:2. Wood mounted on screw chuck, roughed down, and marked out with the parting tool.

Fig. 1:3. Shaping the stem.

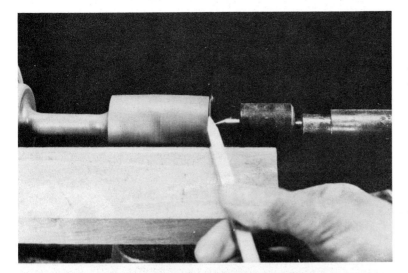

Fig. 1:4. Squaring the end with the long corner of the chisel.

Fig. 1:5. Planing and fining with the skew chisel.

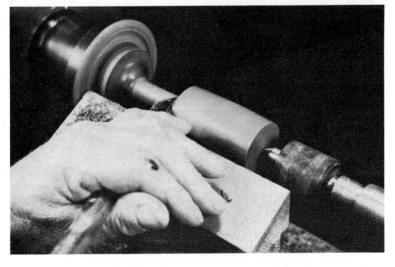

Fig. 1:6. Planing the stem with the ½-in (12.7-mm) skew chisel.

9

Fig. 1:7. Boring the candleholder with the saw-tooth cutter.

Fig. 1:8. Brass insert placed in position.

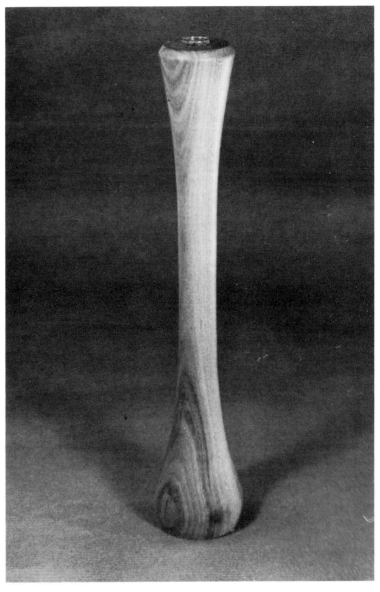

2 Bud Vase

Design Specification

A simple shape, with an inverted glass tube to hold water and receive a single flower (**2:1**).

Wood

Cherry.

Finish

Seal with a sanding sealer. Polish with beeswax.

11

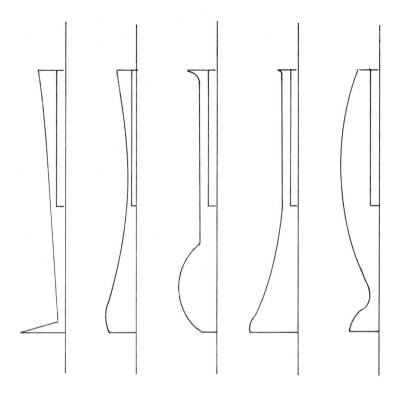

Attachment to the Lathe

Assembled between the screw chuck and revolving center.

Lathe Speed

1400 rpm reduced to 800 rpm when boring.

Tools

Spindle gouges and chisel
Sawtooth or flatbit for boring
Tailstock drill chuck
Screw chuck and revolving center

Method

Straightforward spindle turning.

Turning the Vase

Mount between the screw chuck and the revolving center (**2:2**). This method of holding will allow the revolving center to be removed and the drill chuck substituted for boring to receive the glass insert.

Rough down to size with a gouge (**2:3**). Mark out with a pencil and parting tool. Shape with a roundnose gouge (**2:4**); plane with the skew chisel (**2:5**). Clean up and polish.

Fig. 2:2. Wood mounted on the screw chuck; revolving center brought up for additional support.

Fig. 2:3. Wood mounted between screw chuck and revolving center, roughed down to size with the 1¼-in (32-mm) deep gouge.

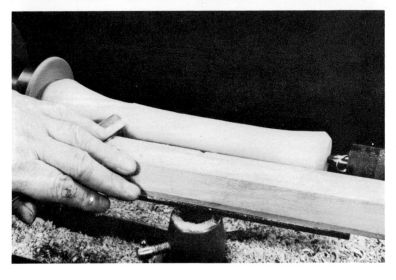

Fig. 2:4. Shaping with the round-nose gouge.

Remove revolving center, place a sawtooth cutter in the drill chuck, reduce the lathe speed to 800 rpm and bore a hole to receive the glass insert (2:6). Unscrew the vase from the lathe and clean up its base by hand, filling the screw hole at the same time.

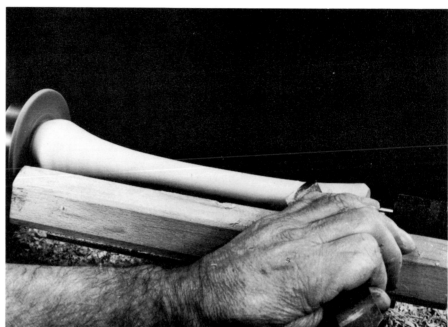

Fig. 2:5. Planing with the skew chisel to obtain a final finish.

Fig. 2:6. Boring with the sawtooth cutter before inserting a glass tube.

Fig. 3:1

3 Dinner Mats

Design Specification
Thin turning (**3:1**), two each of three sizes.

Wood
A laminate made up of constructional veneer of various colors.

Finish
Hand finish—use a two-part acid catalyst.

Attachment to the Lathe
Glue-chuck method.

Lathe Speed
High.

Tools
¼-in or ⅜-in (6.3-mm or 9.6-mm) gouge
Faceplate with glue block

Method

Edge-turned only, using the gouge.

Turning

Glue each disc to the glue chuck (**3:2**) using an electric hot-melt glue gun. (An alternative would be to use the glue-and-paper method; this, however, takes up time waiting for the glue to set, while the hot-melt assembly can be used immediately.) Use the spindle gouge to turn to size, and round each edge over. Finish and polish.

Fig. 3:2. Disc attached to glue chuck.

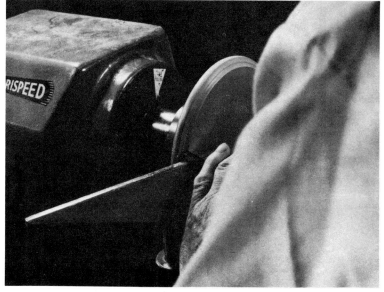

Fig. 3:3. Edge shaping.

4 Coasters

Fig. 4:1. Coaster in black walnut, with inserted center of bog oak.

Design Specification

A simple design for easy cleaning, made from laminated constructional veneers (**4:1**).

Wood

Zebrano (zebra wood), with interleaves of English sycamore.

Finish

A hard heat-resistant polish.

Attachment to the Lathe

Glue-chuck method.

Lathe Speed

1200 rpm.

Tools

⅜-in (9.6-mm) spindle gouge

Method

Using constructional veneers, make up a laminate. Use P.V.A. glue and alternate the grain with each layer. This will provide a more stable laminate. Alternatively, thin wood or a veneer glued to high-quality plywood could be used. Attach the laminate to a prepared glue chuck. Turn down to round and to the desired diameter with a ¼-in (6.3-mm) gouge, carefully rounding over the edge. Clean up, polish and finish. Using a knife, remove carefully from the glue chuck.

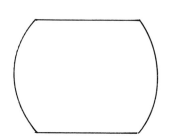

Fig. 5:1

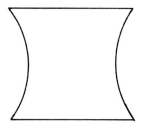

5 Napkin Rings

Design Specification

For distinctions between napkins, it is suggested that the design of each ring should be different. Distinctions could, of course, be attained by the use of different woods. The method suggested here is best suited to the making of three or four at one setting, and is more economical in wood and time (**5:1**).

Wood

Cherry.

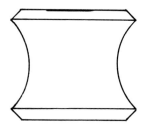

Finish

Two coats of sanding sealer cut back with fine steel wool.

Attachment to the Lathe
Collar chuck or split ring with the six-in-one chuck.

Lathe Speed
1200 rpm.

Tools
¾-in. (19-mm) deep roughing gouge
1-in (2.5-cm) skew chisel
Parting tool
¼-in (6.3-mm) spindle gouge
Collar chuck
Drill chuck
1¼-in (3.2-cm) flatbit (or similar)

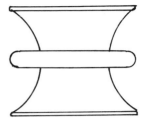

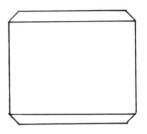

Method
Turn down the selected wood between centers to fit the collar chuck (**5:2**). Remove, place the wood in the collar chuck and screw onto the headstock. Bring up the tailstock to give additional support. Mark out dimensions with a pencil. Use the parting tool to mark up starting points (**5:5**). With the skew chisel and ¼-in (3.2-cm) gouge, shape each ring in turn (**5:6-7**).

The parting tool is used to cut a separation groove between each ring. Cut the groove slightly under the internal diameter of each ring. Using the skew chisel, square up and plane the end of each ring (**5:9**). Clean up and polish.

Fig. 5:2. Wood turned to fit the collar chuck.

Fig. 5:3. Checking the size with the ring of the collar chuck.

Fig. 5:4. Assembling the turned billet in the collar chuck.

Fig. 5:5. Marking out with the parting tool.

Fig. 5:6. Shaping with the ¼-in (6.3-mm) beading gouge.

Fig. 5:7. Shaping with the ½-in (12.7-mm) skew chisel.

Fig. 5:8. Curving with the skew chisel.

Fig. 5:9. Squaring the end of each ring with the long corner of the skew chisel.

Fig. 5:10. Boring with the flatbit.

Fig. 5:11. First ring bored through.

Remove the tailstock, replace the dead center with a drill chuck (**5:10**). Use a ¼-in (3.2-cm) flatbit to bore the center out of each ring. Each one will break off at the parting groove (**5:11**). The stub remaining must be turned down to the inside diameter of the rings with a slight taper from back to front (**5:12**). This is used as a mandrel to remount each ring for final cleaning up and polishing (**5:13**).

The inside of each ring can be cleaned up if necessary, using a small wood chuck into which each ring can be placed.

Fig. 5:12. Placing the napkin ring on the mandrel to trim and curve the inside.

Fig. 5:13. Curving the inside with the scraper.

FIRST COURSE— STARTERS

6   Hors d'Oeuvre Dish

Fig. 6:1. Hors d'oeuvre dish in English walnut on Lazy Susan™ bearing.

Design Specification

A two-piece turning, combined with a Lazy Susan™ unit to create a rotary dish (**6:1**).

Wood

Walnut or any other suitable wood available in large sizes.

Finish

Two coats of white French polish cut back with steel wool to produce a hard eggshell finish.

Attachment to the Lathe

4-in (10-cm) faceplate.

Lathe Speed

700 rpm for the dish.
1200 rpm for the base.

Tools

⅜-in (9.6-mm) long and strong gouge
Parting tool
Flatting scraper
4-in (10-cm) faceplate
Screw chuck

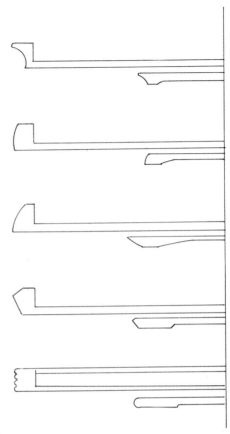

Fig. 6:2. Turning down to round.

Method

Carefully plane the wood from which the dish is to be made. This will avoid the turning of the underside. Attach to the planed face a 4-in (10-cm) left-hand faceplate. Place the wood on the lathe and carefully turn down to the required diameter (**6:2**). Mark out with pencil and parting tool (**6:3**). With the ⅜-in (9.6-mm) gouge, turn the inside to size and shape (**6:4-5**).

Fig. 6:3. Cutting point of start with the parting tool.

Fig. 6:4. Turning the corner with the ¼-in (6.3-mm) roundnose gouge.

26

Fig. 6:5. Turning the disc recess.

Complete, finish and polish. Remove from the lathe. Screw the base piece to the screw chuck. Turn each side separately, and polish. Remove from the lathe and attach the Lazy Susan to complete the dish.

Fig. 7:1. Grapefruit dish in English walnut.

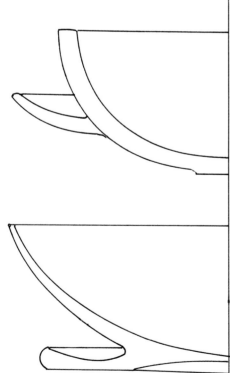

7 Grapefruit Dish

Design Specification
Large enough to hold the average grapefruit, with a rim to receive the seeds (7:1).

Wood
Close-grained hardwood, walnut, or any of the fruit trees.

Finish
Oil finish, preferably mineral oil applied fairly liberally.

Attachment to the Lathe
Glue chuck mounted on a faceplate.

Lathe speed
1200 rpm.

Tools
⅜-in (9.6-mm) long and strong gouge
¼-in (6.3-mm) roundnose gouge
Parting tool

Method

Use the hot-melt glue gun to attach the block to the glue chuck (**7:2**), after first planing the base flat and true. Turn to round with the gouge (**7:3**). Mark out with pencil and parting tool (**7:4**). Begin to shape with the ¼-in (6.3-mm) roundnose gouge (**7:5-6**), first cutting the seed rim (**7:7**). Mark out the bowl limit with the parting tool (**7:8**). Begin to clear the waste with the ⅜-in (9.6-mm) deep long and strong gouge (**7:9-10**). Shape carefully. Cut the edge with the ¼-in (6.3-mm) gouge, taking care to let the bevel rub on the wood for support and a fine finish, moving outward in both directions from the center of the edge (**7:11-12**).

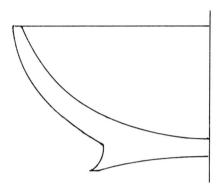

Fig. 7:2. Walnut block glued to chuck and mounted on the lathe.

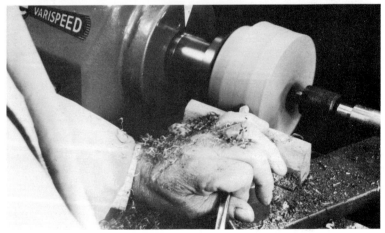

Fig. 7:3. Sizing down with the ¼-in (6.3-mm) gouge.

Fig. 7:4. Marking out with the ⅛-in (3.2-mm) parting tool.

Fig. 7:5. Shaping with the ¼-in (6.3-mm) gouge.

Fig. 7:6. Shaping with the ¼-in (6.3-mm) gouge (continued).

Fig. 7:7. Shaping the seed rim.

Fig. 7:8. Cutting a point of start with the parting tool.

Fig. 7:9. Removing the waste and shaping with the ⅜-in (9.6-mm) long and strong bowl gouge.

Fig. 7:10. Deeping with the ⅜-in (9.6-mm) gouge.

Fig. 7:11. Facing the edge with the ¼-in (6.3-mm) gouge.

Fig. 7:12. Facing the edge with the ¼-in (6.3-mm) gouge (continued).

Clean up with flour-grade sandpaper or a similar paper, if necessary (**7:13**). A fine finish can be obtained with the use of 0000 grade steel wool (**7:14**). Polish by saturating with cooking oil. When the polishing is complete, separate the dish and the glue chuck with a knife. Use a cardboard template to repeat the exact shape if you are going to make others.

Fig. 7:13. Papering the inside.

Fig. 7:14. Final finishing with steel wool.

SECOND COURSE—SOUP

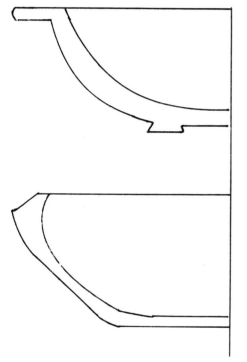

8   Soup Bowl

Fig. 8:1. Soup bowl in teak.

Design Specification

The design should permit stacking to save on storage space.

Wood

Teak.

Finish

A hard polish cut back to a matte finish with steel wool.

Attachment to the Lathe

Expanding collet chuck.

Faceplate.

Lathe Speed

1200 rpm.

Tools

¼-in (6.3-mm) spindle gouge

⅜-in (9.6-mm) long and strong gouge

Parting tool

Method

Attach the faceplate to the prepared block with 1-in No. 8 screws. Tighten the chuck in position and screw to the lathe. Mark out a recess to receive the expanding collet. Using the gouge, shape the outside of the bowl. Clean up, remove the faceplate and reverse, securing the collet in the recess. Remount to the lathe.

Mark out, as previously, with parting tool and gouge. Use the long and strong gouge to remove the waste, and shape. Check carefully that the inside diameter at the top is sized to fit the plinth of the soup bowl which will be turned to fit on top.

Turn two, four or six bowls as required. Apply the finish and set aside to add the handles later.

Fig. 8:2. Shaping the outside with the ⅜-in (9.6-mm) high-speed steel (HSS) gouge.

Fig. 8:3. Shaping.

Fig. 8:4. Using the ⅜-in (9.6-mm) HSS gouge to shape the inside.

Fig. 9:1

9   Bread Dish with Handle

Design Specification

A deep turning with a center pillar which will be sawn through the center and glued end to end so that it forms the dish handle. Wooden studs will serve as feet (**9:1**).

Wood

Sycamore or maple.

Finish

As left from the tools.

Attachment to the Lathe

Faceplate.

Lathe Speed

1000 rpm.

Tools

3-in (7.5-cm) faceplate
1-in (2.5-cm) roughing gouge
⅜-in (9.6-mm) long and strong gouge
Spade scraper

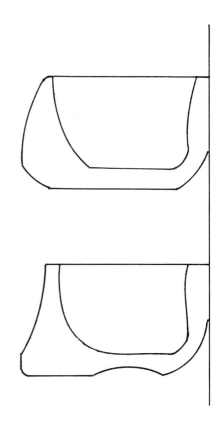

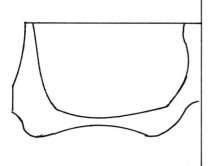

Fig. 9:2. Wood mounted.

Method

On the Lathe—Screw the prepared block to the face-plate (**9:2**). Turn to round. Turn the inside, leaving a center pillar to form a handle. Completely finish the turning. Part off carefully.

On the Bench—With great care, saw the turning exactly in half. Glue the two halves end to end (**9:3**). Then, when the glue is completely hard, carefully plane the top edges of the dish and the handle. Round off the sharp edges with a glass-paper block.

Fig. 9:3. The split turning prior to gluing.

Fig. 10:1

10 Toast Rack

Design Specification

The prerequisite of most of the projects in this book is clean lines to make for easy cleaning. This rule particularly applies to the toast rack (**10:1**).

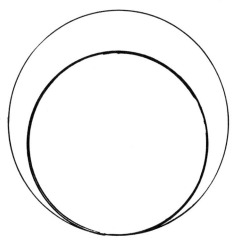

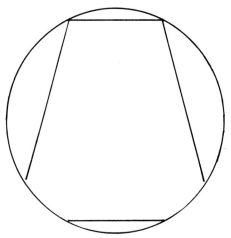

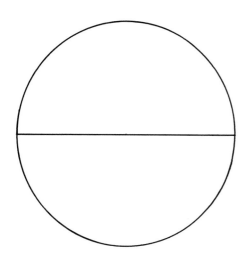

Wood

Close-grained, odorless beech was used, but any wood having these qualities will suffice.

Finish

Wood must be sealed against oil and grease, and it must be easy to clean.

Attachment to the Lathe

These small pieces of wood can be attached to the lathe using the hot-melt glue gun and a glue chuck. Other designs permit the use of a small wood chuck or, with those permitting a center hole, the parts can be mounted on a mandrel.

Lathe Speed

Around 1200-1400 rpm.

Tools

⅜-in (9.6-mm) roundnose spindle gouge
Parting tool

Fig. 10:2. Wood mounted to glue chuck.

Fig. 10:3. Turning with the ⅜-in (9.6-mm) HSS gouge.

Method

Prepare the wood by accurately planing to final thickness before cutting into discs. Cut a small block of wood for the glue chuck, slightly less in diameter than the pre-cut discs. Screw the block to a screw chuck or small faceplate.

Use the hot-melt glue gun to attach each disc (**10:2**), and turn down each one accurately to size with the spindle gouge (**10:3**). Shape carefully and bring to a final finish.

Assemble the base disc to the screw chuck, turn down to round and shape, again with the ¼-in (6.3-mm) round-nose gouge. Bring to a finish and remove from the lathe.

Carefully mark out the base, saw off the sides, and plane.

Mark a center line, bore five ³/₁₆-in (5-mm) holes to locate each standing disc. Similarly bore a ³/₁₆-in (5-mm) hole in each disc. Cut dowels and finally assemble with glue. Carefully touch up with fine paper or steel wool, and oil with cooking oil to complete the job.

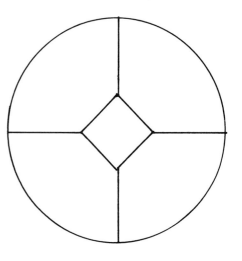

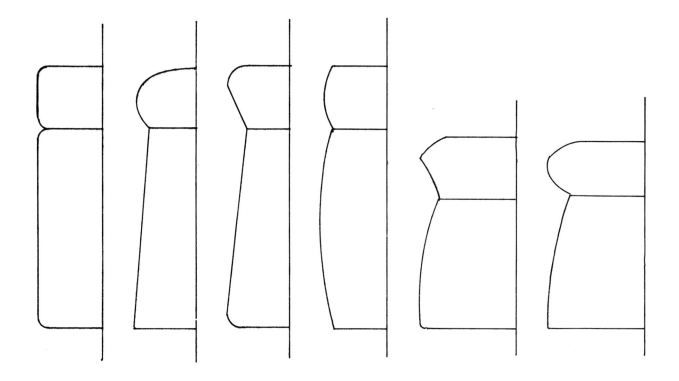

11 Pepper Mill

Design Specification
The size of the mill will be dictated by the mechanism available. Care in design will be needed to ensure a good hand grip for both the body and top. The mill must also be easy to clean.

Wood
Teak.

Finish
Oil.

Attachment to the Lathe
A collar chuck or expanding collet chuck.

Lathe Speed
1200 rpm.

Tools

    ¾-in (19-mm) roughing gouge
    1-in (2.5-cm) skew chisel
    Parting tool
    Spindle gouge

Method (see photos of turning a salt mill, pp. 81-88)

Prepare the wood between centers so that it can be held in the collar chuck (see page 82 for details). Screw the assembly to the lathe and bring up the tailstock. Plane to size. Mark out with pencil and parting tool. Shape both body and top.

Cut a rabbet on the body top. When finally assembled, the body will fit in a recess in the top. Remove the tailstock and replace it with the drill chuck.

Bore to a depth of ½-in (12.7-mm) using a 1½-in (3.8-cm) flatbit. Follow with a 1¼-in (3.2-cm) flatbit, boring to a depth of ⅛-in (3.2-mm) to receive the lip of the body of the mill mechanism, and to a depth of ½-in (12.7-mm) with the ⅞-in (22-mm) flatbit to receive the body.

With a ¾-in (19-mm) flatbit, completely bore the body; the bit should just break into the waste wood between the body and top. Clean up the inside of the body if necessary; part off. Using a 1¼-in (3.2-cm) flatbit, bore a recess ³⁄₁₆-in (5-mm) deep. Follow with a ¾-in (19-mm) flatbit to bore a recess ⅛-in (3.2-mm) deep to receive the mechanism-actuating plate. Finally, with a ³⁄₁₆-in (5-mm) drill, bore a hole completely through the top. This hole will receive the pillar of the mill mechanism.

Complete by parting off the head, using a skew chisel to part into the pillar hole to effect a clean, polished finish on the top. Assemble the mill and screw the locking bar into place in the base to hold the mechanism in place.

Fig. 12:1

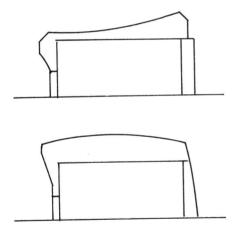

12 Salt and Pepper Shakers

Design Specification
A simple design, with a rubber stopper to enclose the base.

Wood
Teak, enough for both shakers.

Finish
Oil.

Attachment to the Lathe
Collar chuck. Turn down the wood between centers, as shown on page 82, to fit the chuck.

Lathe Speed
1400 rpm for turning.
1000 rpm for boring.

Tools

Roughing gouges
1-in (2.5-cm) skew chisel
¾-in (19-mm) and 1-in (2.5-cm) sawtooth cutter
Tailstock drill chuck
Collar chuck

Method

Screw the collar chuck to the lathe. Tighten down the collar to hold securely. Bring up the tailstock. Using the 1-in (2.5-cm) skew chisel, turn down the cylinder to size. Mark out with a pencil and follow with the narrow parting tool. Shape with gouge and chisel (12:2-3).

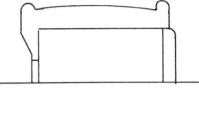

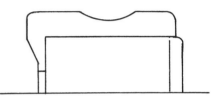

Fig. 12:2. Squaring the top with the skew chisel.

Fig. 12:3. Shaping with the gouge.

Withdraw the tailstock, insert the drill chuck and bore out the base to a depth of ⅜-in (9.6-mm), using the 1-in (2.5-cm) sawtooth machine bit or flatbit (**12:4**). Bore to full depth, i.e., to within ¼-in (6.3-mm) of the top of the box. Clean up, polish (**12:5**) and part off the first box. Shape, bore and complete the second box.

Bore a ¹⁄₁₆-in (1.6-mm) hole in the top of the salt box and five ¹⁄₁₆-in (1.6-mm) holes in the top of the pepper box, using the bench drill. Seal the inside of both boxes with an acid-catalyst sealer. Fit a rubber or plastic stopper. The salt and pepper shakers are now ready for use.

Fig. 12:4. Boring the body hole with the sawtooth cutter.

Fig. 12:5. Polishing.

THIRD COURSE—
MAIN DISH

13   Dinner Plates
and Side Plates

Fig. 13:1. Dinner or side plate in English walnut, depending upon the size you make it.

Design Specification

Matched plates that will be easy to clean (**13:1**).

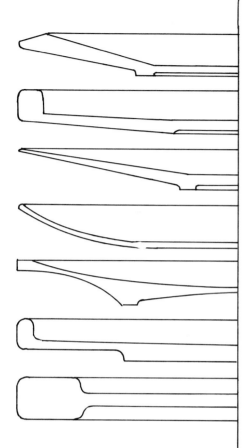

Wood

Hard, close-grained wood; any of the fruit woods; also maple, sycamore, elm or beech.

Finish

Oil.

Attachment to the Lathe

Attached to the screw chuck to turn the underside, then reversed into a wood chuck to complete.

Lathe Speed

1000-1400 rpm, depending upon the size of the plate.

Tools

Parting tools
¼-in (6.3-mm) spindle gouge
⅜-in (9.6-mm) deep long and strong gouge
1-in (2.5-cm) flatting scraper chisel

Method

Making the Wood Chuck—Mount a block of softwood to faceplate. Turn down to round.

Place the tee rest across the face and cut a recess the exact size of the plate. A slight taper from front to back will assist the fit of the plate (**13:2**).

Cut a hole right through the center of the block. This will assist in the removal of the plate, should there be any difficulty.

Making the Plate—Screw the prepared disc to the screw chuck, but place two discs of ⅛-in (3.2-mm) hardboard between the face of the chuck and the disc to reduce the amount of penetration of the screw into the wood (**13.3**).

Use the gouge to turn down to the correct diameter (**13:4-5**).

Mark out the underside with pencil and parting tool. The ⅜-in (9.6-mm) deep long and strong gouge can be used to shape the plate. Careful cutting can produce a perfect finish, but an imperfect one can be finalized with a scraper. Take care to trail the tool and take only fine shavings. Complete by papering, including the edge. Oil and remove from the screw chuck.

Place the wood chuck on the lathe and carefully insert the half-completed plate, finished side inwards (**13:6**). A good push-fit is all that is needed. Bring up the tool rest

Fig. 13:2. Hollowing out the chuck.

Fig. 13:3. Disc and screw chuck (finished chuck on the right).

Fig. 13:4. Turning down to correct diameter.

completely across the plate and as close to the work as possible, slightly above center. Should the plate loosen, it cannot come out (13:7). Mark out with pencil and parting tool. Use the ⅜-in (9.6-mm) deep long and strong gouge to shape the plate (13:8-9). Finish as before.

Make each plate, using the same chuck. To obtain exact replicas, make a cardboard template for checking.

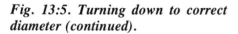
Fig. 13:5. Turning down to correct diameter (continued).

Fig. 13:6. Part-finished plate inserted into prepared wood chuck.

Fig. 13:7. Mounted on the lathe.

Fig. 13:8. Cutting with the ⅜-in (9.6-mm) HSS gouge.

Fig. 13:9. Cutting continued.

Fig. 14:1. Side salad bowl in teak.

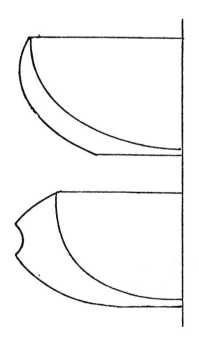

14　Side Salad Bowls

Design Specification
An uncomplicated shape, with the dish standing on a firm base to establish solidity when cutting and eating the salad (**14:1**). The requirements are one large salad bowl and six side salad dishes.

Wood
Teak or any of the fruit trees.

Finish
Cooking oil or an acid catalyst finish to seal against moisture.

Attachment to the Lathe
Since six or more dishes will be required, it will be best

to use an expanding collet chuck. The Coronet type will be found most suitable since it is extremely accurate and trouble-free in use.

Lathe Speed

1000-1200 rpm.

Tools

⅜-in (9.6-mm) long and strong gouge
Parting tool
¼-in (6.3-mm) roundnose spindle gouge

Method

Prepare the blanks and attach to either a faceplate or a screw chuck. Place on the lathe, bring up the tool rest across the end of the blank and quickly turn down to round with the ⅜-in (9.6-mm) gouge (**14:2-3**). Change the tool rest to across the base of the work and mark a recess with the parting tool (**14:4**). This recess should be just under the expanded size of the collet chuck in diameter (**14:5**).

Turn out the waste inside the recess with the ¼-in (6.3-mm) roundnose gouge (**14:6**) and, when complete, use the long corner of the ½-in (12.7-mm) skew chisel to under-cut the recess (**14:7**), giving it a dovetail angle to receive the expanding collet.

Change to the ⅜-in (9.6-mm) long and strong gouge and, working from the inside towards the outside, shape the underside of the bowl (**14:8**). Bring to a final finish and remove from the lathe.

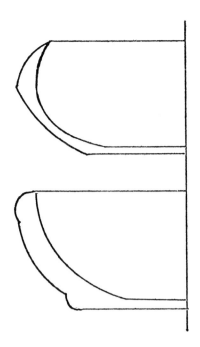

Fig. 14:2. Turning blank to size.

53

Fig. 14:3. Using the ⅜-in (9.6-mm) Woodcraft gouge to turn to round.

Fig. 14:4. Marking size of recess with the parting tool.

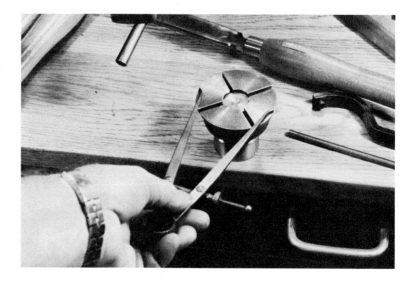

Fig. 14:5. Taking chuck collet size.

Fig. 14:6. Removing waste with the ¼-in (6.3-mm) roundnose gouge.

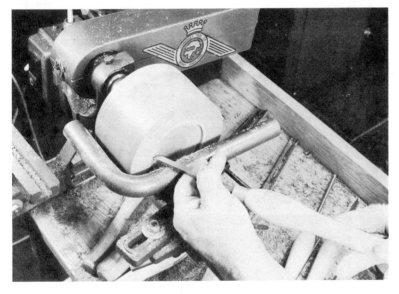

Fig. 14:7. Undercutting the recess with the long corner of the ½-in (12.7-mm) skew chisel.

Unscrew the faceplate and insert the Coronet expanding collet into the prepared recess (14:9). Tighten firmly and return to the lathe (14:10). Place the tool rest in position across the face of the bowl and slightly below center. Use the parting tool to make a groove at the limit of internal diameter. This groove will also act as a starting point for the gouge. Use the ¼-in (6.3-mm) roundnose gouge to bore a hole in the center of the bowl to give an indication of the final depth.

Take the ⅜-in (9.6-mm) long and strong gouge and, starting from the groove, with the bevel "looking at" the wood and resting on it, begin to remove the waste. Keep the right hand well down, but raise the gouge, keeping the bevel in the same plane as it moves towards the center of the bowl, in order to be sure that the gouge will cut into the exact center of the bowl (**14:11**).

Fig. 14:8. Shaping with the ⅜-in (9.6-mm) long and strong gouge.

Fig. 14:9. Outside of bowl completed; inserting the chuck.

Fig. 14:10. Chuck tightened.

Fig. 14:11. Shaping the inside with the ⅜-in (9.6-mm) long and strong gouge.

Fig. 14:12. Finishing cut with the ⅜-in (9.6-mm) Woodcraft gouge.

57

Progressively remove the waste, cutting down to arrive at a fine edge and a good finish (**14:12**). Clean up (**14:13**) and polish with a good brand of cooking oil.

Use a template when cutting both inside and outside to ensure the bowls are a good match. The larger salad bowl will be exactly alike in design and turned in the same way.

An alternative method of holding would be to turn the underside of each dish, leaving a small plinth as a base. This could then be pushed into a wood chuck for holding when turning the inside of each bowl.

Fig. 14:13. Finishing with steel wool.

15 Goblet

Fig. 15:1. Goblet in walnut.

Design Specification

Wine vessel, thin wall, pedestal design (**15:1**).

Wood

Any fruit wood.

Finish

A hard catalyst finish.

Attachment to the Lathe

Faceplate.

Lathe Speed

1200-1400 rpm.

Tools

Screw chuck
¼-in (6.3-mm) gouge
⅜-in (9.6-mm) long and strong gouge
½-in (12.7-mm) spindle gouge
Parting tools
Tailstock chuck
1½-in (3.75-cm) sawtooth cutter

Method

Prepare the selected wood, accurately square one end and screw it to the faceplate. Place on the lathe, bring up the tailstock and turn to round **(15:2)**. Mark out. Use the parting tool to mark starting points in order to use the gouge for shaping **(15:3)**.

Fig. 15:2. Planing to round.

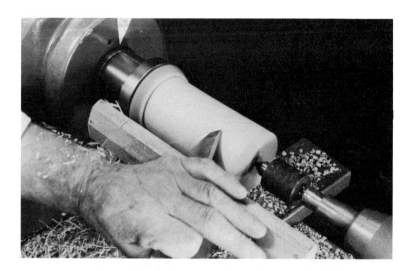

Fig. 15:3. Marking points of start with the parting tool.

Remove the tailstock, place the tool rest across the face of the goblet, mark a starting point with the parting tool **(15:4)**. Place the sawtooth cutter in the tailstock chuck and bore out as much of the work as possible. Remove the cutter, bring up the tool rest and use the ⅜-in (9.6-mm) long and strong gouge to shape the inside of the bowl **(15:5)**.

With the bowl complete, return the tool rest to spindle-turning position and use the ¼- and ½-in (6.3- and 12.7-mm) spindle-turning gouges to shape the outside of the bowl, base and stem **(15:6-9)**.

Fig. 15:4. Cutting points of start for the gouge with the parting tool.

Fig. 15:5. Cutting the inside of the bowl.

Fig. 15:6. Roughing the outside.

Fig. 15:7. Shaping.

Fig. 15:8. Shaping the base.

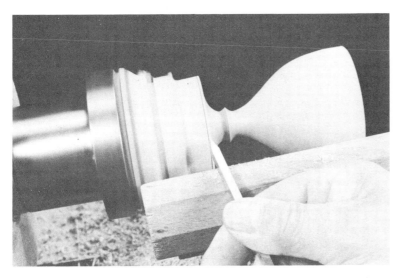

Complete the finish as necessary. Polish. Part off and clean up the base on an abrasive board. Turn each goblet separately, using a template to check each one for accuracy in shape and size. Alternatively, the work could be held on a small faceplate or mounted in a collar chuck.

It is not absolutely necessary to remove the bulk of the waste by boring, but this will save time and it is much easier than cutting end-grain with the gouge.

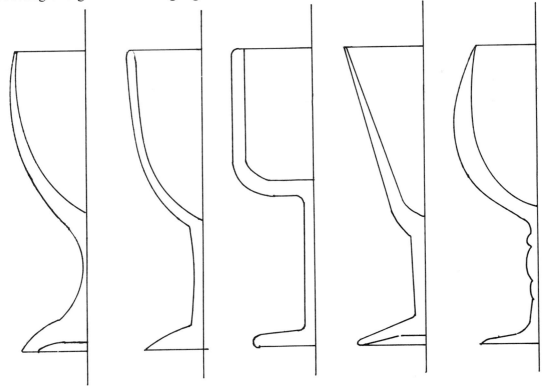

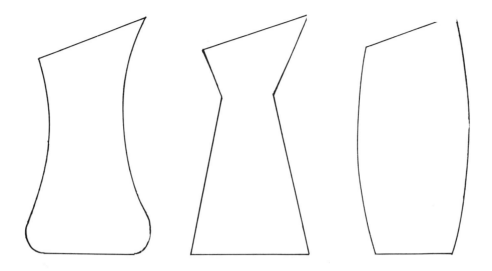

Fig. 16:1. Carafe in elm.

16   Carafe

Design Specification
Designed to be held in the hand without handle. Capacity one pint **(16:1)**.

Wood
Cherry.

Finish
Seal with an acid catalyst finish.

Attachment to the Lathe
Faceplate.

Lathe Speed
1200 rpm for cutting.
500 rpm when boring.

Tools

3-in (7.5-cm) faceplate

¾-in (19-mm) deep gouge or 1-in (2.5-cm) roughing gouge

2½-in (6.3-cm) sawtooth machine bit

Parting tool

Spade scraping chisel

Method

Screw the prepared block to the faceplate. Place it on the lathe and bring up the tailstock (16:2). Rough down to size with the ¾-in (19-mm) deep gouge. Shape with gouge and chisel (16:3-5).

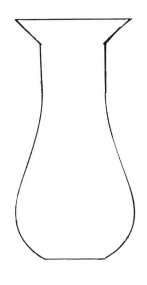

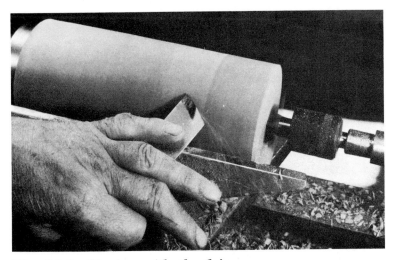

Fig. 16:2. Wood ready for turning.

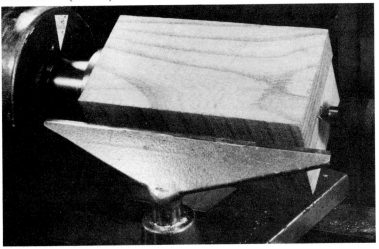

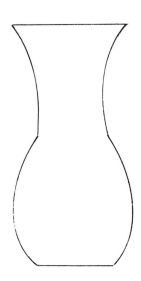

Fig. 16:3. Planing with the 1-in (25.4-mm) chisel.

Fig. 16:4. Shaping with the gouge.

Fig. 16:5. Cutting the mouth of the carafe with the ⅜-in (9.6-mm) HSS gouge.

Remove the tailstock, and replace the center with a drill chuck. Insert the 2½-in (6.3-cm) sawtooth machine bit, and reduce the lathe speed to 500 rpm (**16:6**). Remove the tool rest. With the lathe still, bring up the cutter and carefully mark the center with its brad point. Secure the tailstock; start the lathe.

Hold the chuck with the left hand and wind the cutter into the wood with the right hand. (The chuck hold is only necessary at the beginning of the cut to prevent any possibility of the chuck spinning.) Cut to the correct depth. Replace the tool rest across the face of the job and clean the inside of the carafe with the spade scraper (**16:7**). Open up its mouth (**16:8**).

Fig. 16:6. Boring out with the saw-tooth cutter.

Fig. 16:7. Cleaning up the inside with a scraper.

Fig. 16:8. Opening out the mouth of the carafe.

Stop the lathe, carefully saw the top of the carafe to the correct angle with a tenon saw. Clean up the edge. Polish and part off.

Fig. 17:1

17 Salad Servers

Design Specification
A turning and carving exercise in which, again, the need for simplicity is evident (**17:1**).

Wood
English yew or any strong and pliant hardwood having no odor.

Finish
Any good-quality cooking oil.

Attachment to the Lathe
Centers or cores.

Lathe Speed
1500 rpm.

Tools
¾-in (19-mm) deep standard gouge
¼- and ½-in (6.3- and 12.7-mm) spindle gouge
Parting tool

Method

You will be well advised to consider the servers as a pair throughout the turning, changing the design only during carving. The blanks can be glued together with brown paper between them, or a hot-melt glue gun can be used without the paper. They will separate easily when the turning is complete. The ends of the blanks must be accurately marked for centering on the lathe.

An alternative method that causes no trouble at all would be to use the Coronet cone centers (**17:2**). These substitute for the driving fork and running center and permit the assembly of single pieces, twos in the case of salad servers, or fours. If, for any reason, the pieces have to be returned to the lathe after finalizing, they can be replaced in the cones without loss of centricity.

The carving of the bowls can take place before turning, when the wood is in the flat and is easier to hold. The fork tines can be done when all else is complete.

Turning

Rough down to round with the ¾-in (19-mm) roughing gouge (**17:3**); plane with the 1-in (2.5-cm) skew chisel. Mark out with the parting tool and use both ½- and ¼-in (12.7- and 6.3-mm) spindle gouges to shape the handle and bowl (**17:4**). Take care to bring the handles to a fine section.

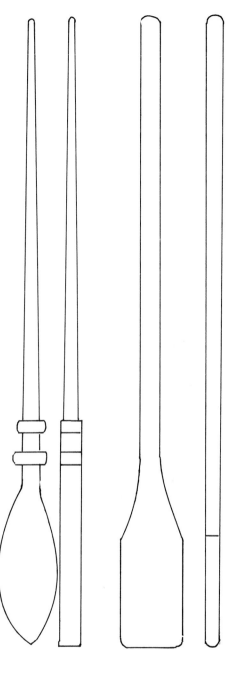

Fig. 17:2. Two pieces placed in the Coronet cone centers.

Fig. 17:3. Roughing with the ¾-in (19-mm) gouge.

Fig. 17:4. Shaping with the spindle gouge.

Finish as necessary, remove from the lathe and separate (17:5-6). Mark out the tines of the fork, cut with the coping saw and clean up with chisel and spokeshave the inside curves of the handles. Oil to complete.

An alternative method of turning would be separate turnings carried out between centers using flat material, turning the handle round, leaving the bowl shaped but still flat, and carving the bowl last.

Fig. 17:5. Lathe work completed.

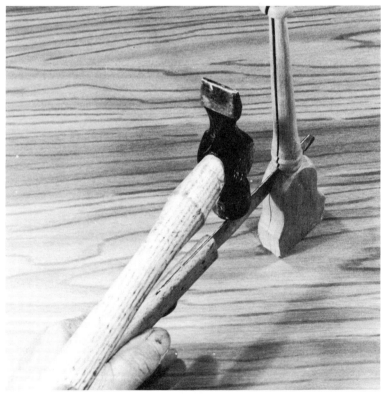

Fig. 17:6. Servers separated.

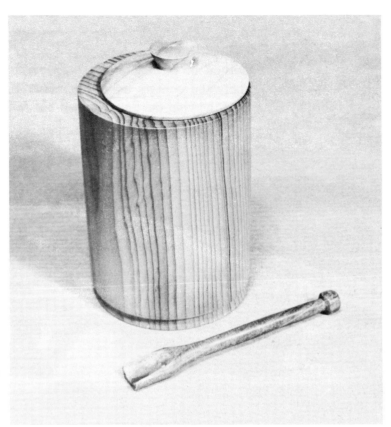

Fig. 18:1

18   Mustard Pot

Design Specification
An easily cleaned turning with an offset bowl.

Wood
Walnut.

Finish
Oiled finish.

Attachment to the Lathe
Electric glue-chuck method. Spoon turned between centers, using square-hole mandrel instead of driving fork.

Lathe Speed

1400 rpm.

Tools

¼-in (6.3-mm) spindle gouge
Sawtooth cutter
Faceplate or screw chuck to hold the glue block

Method

Turned completely to size, but offset for boring.

Turning

The Body—Attach the disc of prepared timber by gluing. Turn to size and shape. Clean up and polish. Remove from the glue chuck and re-assemble, offsetting the required amount. Place tailstock chuck in the tailstock, insert sawtooth cutter and bore recess to receive the glass insert. Clean up and remove.

The Lid—Glue disc to the chuck and use the small gouge to size and shape both lid and knob. Clean up and polish. Remove the lid from the glue with a thin knife.

The Spoon—Mount between centers. Rough down, and shape with gouge and chisel. Clean up and polish. To complete the turning, use a small gouge to shape the bowl inside and cut the spoon-handle recess in the body.

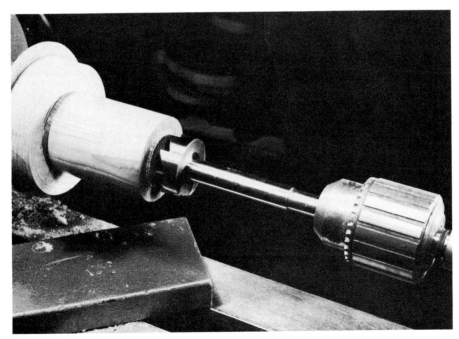

Fig. 18:2. Preparing to use the sawtooth cutter.

Fig. 19:1

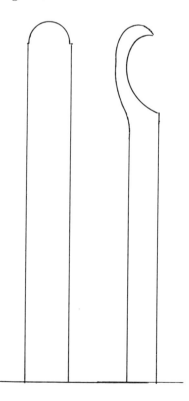

19 Carving Board

Design Specification

The perfect carving board has not yet been designed. Certain features are necessary, particularly the safe containment of the roast when carving, a receptacle for the juices and a solid base on which the dish stands (**19:1**).

Wood

Use teak or one of the fruit-tree woods.

Finish

A good cooking oil, or the wood could be left raw.

Attachment to the Lathe

This design calls for a recess on the underside into

which a disc of cork or rubber is fitted. The cork will prevent the dish from moving when meat is being carved. The Coronet expanding chuck will be ideal for this particular project.

Lathe Speed

1000 rpm.

Tools

Expanding collet chuck
⅜-in (9.6-mm) long and strong bowl gouge
Parting tool
¼-in (6.3-mm) roundnose spindle gouge

Method

Screw the prepared blank to a small faceplate. Bring up the tool rest and, using the ⅜-in (9.6-mm) gouge, turn the blank to round. Place the tool rest across the disc, mark out the recess with the parting tool and, with the bevel running on the wood, remove the waste. Use a ½-in (12.7-mm) skew chisel on its side to slightly undercut the side of the recess to receive the expanding collet chuck.

Complete the shaping of the underside with the gouge and bring to a final finish, as necessary. Remove the work from the lathe, unscrew the faceplate, insert the expanding collet chuck and return the work to the lathe. Once again, place the tool rest across the face of the board and, using the gouge, complete the shaping. Bring to a finish and remove the chuck.

Five small holes, one in the center and four others equi-spaced around, are now bored to receive five studs which will serve to hold the roast in place. The studs used were those used on golf and other sports shoes; they have a thread which turns easily into a bored hole.

Alternative Method of Holding the Board

A block of suitable wood secured to a faceplate should have a recess turned in it exactly the size of the board. The prepared board disc is then inserted into this recess ready for turning.

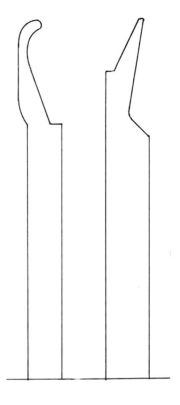

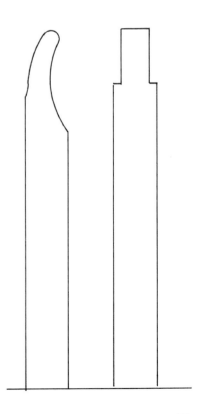

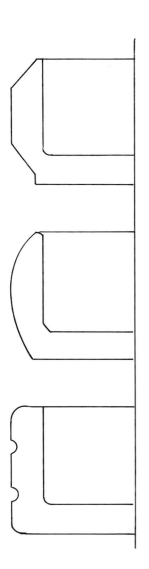

Fig. 20:1

20 Sauce-Bottle Holder with Lid

Design Specification

A design to make the ordinary sauce bottle a more acceptable article on the table. Most makes have round bottles and metal tops. The latter can be glued into the wooden lid; a cork can also be fitted into a lid (**20:1**).

Wood

Any wood will be suitable. Use can be made of the odd pieces from the exotic-wood scrap box.

Finish

Hard polish.

Attachment to the Lathe

Screw chuck/glue chuck.

Lathe Speed

1200-1400 rpm.

Tools

Screw chuck with a wooden block screwed on to make a glue chuck.

Sawtooth machine bit or flatbit of a size to suit the bottle lid and bottle base. Alternatively, the base boring can be omitted and the recess cut with gouge and scraper.

1-in (2.5-cm) skew chisel

¼-in and ½-in (6.3-mm and 12.7-mm) spindle gouge

Method

The Body—Attach the piece for the holder to the glue chuck (**20:2-3**). Turn to round and shape with chisel and gouge (**20:4**). Remove the inside with either the gouge or a boring bit mounted in the tailstock. Clean up, polish and part off.

The Lid—Use the glue chuck as with the body and follow the same procedure (**20:5-10**). An alternative method of holding would be to make a wood chuck from a piece of softwood into which the turned blanks could be inserted for boring out and shaping the top of the lid and the underside of the holder.

Fig. 20:2. Glue gun and glue chuck, with prepared blanks.

77

Another option is to hold each piece on the screw chuck and part off when turning is completed. The parted end in each case may then need a little attention before final polishing.

Fig. 20:3. Body blank secured to glue chuck.

Fig. 20:4. Using the gouge.

Fig. 20:5. Lid—turning with the gouge.

Fig. 20:6. Top—shaping with the gouge.

Fig. 20:7. Marking out the recess with the parting tool and gouge.

Fig. 20:8. Cutting the bottle-top recess.

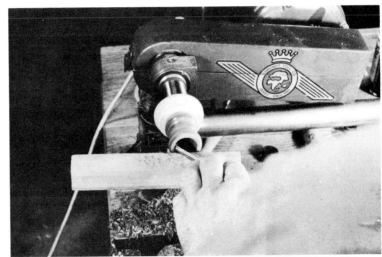

Fig. 20:9. Completing the recess.

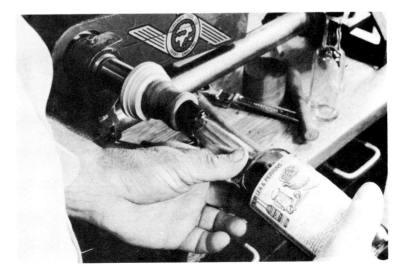

Fig. 20:10. Checking the lid for fit.

Fig. 21:1

21 Salt Mill

Design Specification

This mill is, of course, designed for use with coarse, or kosher, salt. The size of the mill will be determined by the mill mechanism. Mechanisms are available in sizes of 4-12 in. The design must allow the mill to be gripped easily and the head or top rotated without effort. An easily cleaned shape is desirable (**21:1**).

Wood

This should be selected with care; wood with a notice-able smell or with an oil secretion which may contaminate or cause a chemical reaction with the salt should be avoided.

Finish

Seal the wood with a hard sealer or vegetable oil.

Attachment to the Lathe

The collar chuck will be best since it holds the wood securely, particularly when boring. Alternatively, the wood can be held on the screw chuck, but put in an extra screw for safety.

Lathe Speed

1200-1400 rpm.

Tools

¾-in (19-mm) deep standard gouge
½-in and 1-in (12.7-mm and 2.5-cm) skew chisels
¼-in (6.3-mm) roundnose gouge
$^{15}/_{16}$-in and 1¼-in (2.4-cm and 3-cm) flatbits
$^{3}/_{16}$-in (5-mm) wood drill

Method

Mount the blank between centers (**21:2**) and turn down with a flange at one end so that the wood can be secured in the collar chuck. Use the Coronet collet chuck, which accepts smaller wood than the six-in-one.

Secure the turned blank in the collet chuck, i.e., without the collet, and attach to the lathe. Using the 1-in (2.5-cm) skew chisel, plane the blank to size as necessary. Mark out with the pencil and parting tool and allow ⅜-in (9.6-mm) of waste between the body and the top or head of the mill (**21:3-4**).

Fig. 21:2. Two blanks prepared between centers; one blank inserted in the collet chuck.

Fig. 21:3. Marking out with the pencil.

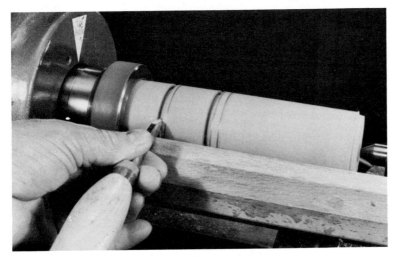

Fig. 21:4. Marking out with the parting tool.

With the chisel and gouge, shape the body and top (**21:5-8**). With the parting tool, cut a rabbet in the body just below the point of parting (the top will drop over this when the mill is assembled). Secure a drill chuck in the tailstock and drop in a 1¼-in (3.1-cm) flatbit. Secure the tailstock with the flatbit point almost touching the wood. Run the lathe and carefully advance the bit—bore to a depth of ¼-in (6.3-mm) (**21:9**). Remove the flatbit and replace with a 1-in (2.5-cm) flatbit, then carefully bore another hole 3¾-in (9.5-cm) deep. Remove the tailstock assembly, completely finish the body, replace the tool rest and part off the body. The parting tool will cut into the hole you just drilled.

Again, bring up the tailstock and place a 1¼-in (3.1-cm) flatbit in position. Bore a recess in the top to a depth of ¼-in (6.3-m). Replace with a 1-in (2.5-cm) flatbit and bore a ⅛-in

(3.2-mm) recess to receive the actuating plate of the mill (**21:10**). Finally, with a ³/₁₆-in (5-mm) wood drill, bore a hole right through the head (**21:11**).

Finish cutting and finishing the top, and part off into the ³/₁₆-in (5-mm) hole (**21:12**). Apply the final finish to both parts.

Fig. 21:5. Shaping with the chisel.

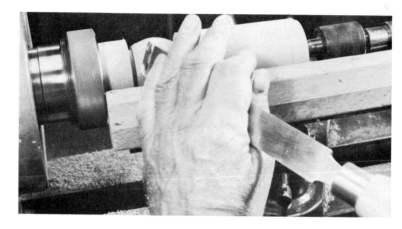

Fig. 21:6. Shaping to a taper with the 1-in (25.4-mm) skew chisel.

Fig. 21:7. Shaping with the skew chisel.

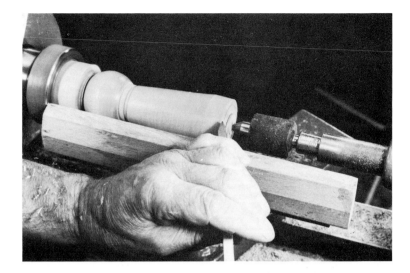

Fig. 21:8. Squaring the base with the long corner of the ½-in (12.7-mm) skew chisel.

Fig. 21:9. Boring the body with a 1¼-in (32-mm) flatbit.

Fig. 21:10. Boring the recess to receive the actuating plate.

Fig. 21:11. Using the wood drill to cut the shaft hole.

Fig. 21:12. Parting off the top with the skew chisel.

To Assemble

Insert the body of the mill into the base and secure it with two small brass screws (**21:13**). Pass the cutter and rod through the body (**21:14-15**). Using two small screws, fix the actuating plate in the head (**21:16**). Place body and head together, pushing the rod through the top and finally screwing down the brass knob. Do not screw down too tightly—the top should rotate freely. The best salt-mill mechanisms are those having a nylon body and grinder.

Fig. 21:13. Body inserted to be screwed into place.

Fig. 21:14. Inserting the cutter and rod.

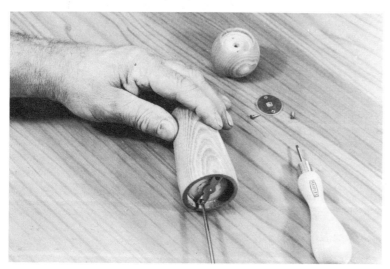

Fig. 21:15. Screwing the tie bar in place.

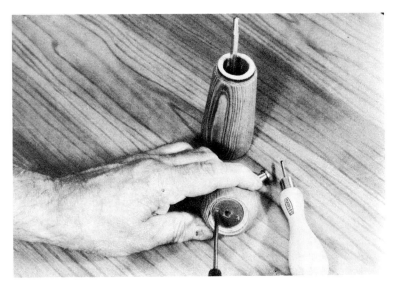

Fig. 21:16. Screwing the actuating plate in place.

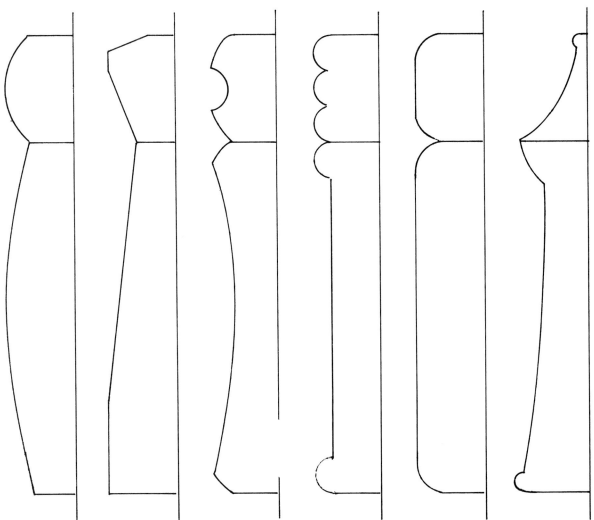

22 Wine Bottle

Design Specification

Any bottle from which drink will be served must be shaped to provide a good hand grip. At the same time, the mouth must be capable of passing the wine smoothly into the goblet. There are already many attractive shapes in glass from which the turner may gain inspiration (**22:1**).

Wood

A piece of carefully selected, mature oak would be fine for this exercise, although chestnut could be substituted.

American oak has always been considered best for wine, but Baltic oak is recommended for beer.

Finish

The outside of the bottle should be sealed and could be brought to a high finish, if so desired. The polish must, however, be impervious to moisture.

Fig. 22:1

Attachment to the Lathe

Turned between centers; only the driving fork and running center will be needed.

Lathe Speed

1200 rpm.

Tools

¾-in (19-mm) deep standard gouge
1-in (2.5-cm) skew chisel
½-in (12.7-mm) spindle gouge
Parting tool

Method

Unlike most of our turned projects, this one starts as a carving. The selected board is accurately planed and the inside shape is marked out on the face. Use a template for this; the same template can be used to check the shape of the outside.

Using a quick-carving gouge, with the wood held firmly on the bench top, shape out the inside of the bottle. Use a slow gouge to bring the work to a smooth finish. Carefully glue up the two halves. When the glue is dry, accurately locate the centers and place the block on the lathe (22:2). Using the ¾-in (19-mm) gouge, rough down to round and shape with the ½-in (12.7-mm) spindle gouge. In the particular design shown, the curves were finished with the 1-in (2.5-cm) skew chisel (22:3-4).

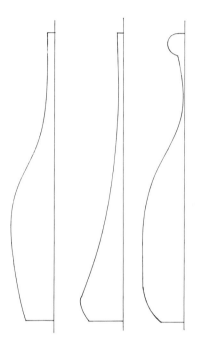

Fig. 22:2. Bottle carved internally, glued up and mounted between centers.

Completely finish, including polish. Part the work off, cleaning off the bottom if necessary, although this should have been hollowed slightly, leaving only the pip to be removed. Select a suitably sized sawtooth cutter to bore the mouth of the bottle. Do this with the bench drill.

The Stopper—A cork should be used to close the bottle, but for table use a small wooden stopper should be turned.

Again use matching oak, turn between centers or use the Coronet collet chuck to hold the wood. This will be a simple exercise in turning with the small gouge and chisel.

Fig. 22:3. Planing to shape with the 1-in (25-mm) skew chisel.

Fig. 22:4. Ready for polishing.

FOURTH COURSE— DESSERT

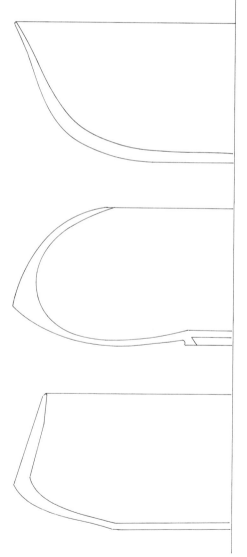

23   Fruit Bowl

Design Specification

Smooth curves must be the order of the day. The design must also permit thin walls, otherwise a deep bowl like this one will be extremely cumbersome in use (**23:1**).

Wood

A large piece may well prove difficult to find. Ideally, use teak or one of the fruit woods, but less likely ones could be used as long as the one selected will not in any way contaminate the fruit or be affected by the juices.

Finish

Leave it natural if possible; otherwise, seal with a two-part acid catalyst mix and cut back with steel wool to give a matte finish.

Attachment to the Lathe

Faceplate and expanding collet chuck.

Lathe Speed

1000 rpm.

Tools

⅜-in (9.6-mm) long and strong bowl gouge
¼-in (6.3-mm) roundnose spindle gouge
Parting tool

Method

The outside or underside of the bowl is first turned by assembling the blank to a faceplate. A recess to receive the expanding collet chuck is cut (**23:2**), as with earlier projects. With the underside complete (**23:3**), the job is reassembled to the collet chuck and returned to the lathe.

Bring up the tee rest close to the work and slightly

Fig. 23:2. Finishing the dovetail recess to receive the chuck.

below center. Use the parting tool to mark the diameter limit and to provide a groove to use as a starting point for the gouge (**23:4**). Take the ¼-in (6.3-mm) roundnose spindle gouge to bore a hole in the center to provide an indication of depth.

Using the ⅜-in (9.6-mm) deep long and strong gouge, with the bevel "looking at" the wood and right hand well down, proceed to remove the waste (**23:5**). Remember to raise the right hand, but at the same time maintain the cut, to make sure that the center of the gouge will in fact finish at

Fig. 23:3. Underside completed.

Fig. 23:4. Marking the limit of the diameter with the parting tool.

the center of the bowl. Quite strong cuts can be taken, but the final cuts should be fine to produce a good surface finish (23:6).

Complete as the surface dictates and polish if necessary.

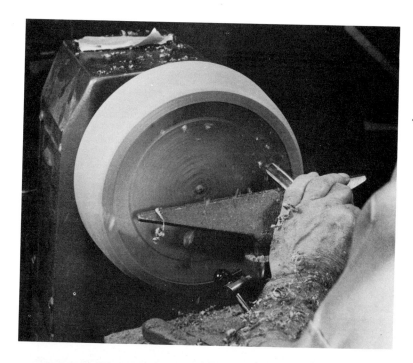

Fig. 23:5. Removing the waste with the ⅜-in (9.6-mm) long and strong gouge.

Fig. 23:6. Finishing cuts.

24   Fruit Dish

Design Specification

A single-ring design specifically to hold oranges, apples, and other fresh fruit (**24:1**).

Wood

Walnut or any fruit wood.

Finish

Sanding sealer and wax.

Attachment to the Lathe

Two methods are suggested. The old craftsman would mount the blank on a faceplate and turn the underside complete to the rim, polish and finish. Having first prepared his wood chuck, he would now push the work into the recess in the chuck and turn the inside. This is a sound method and one which I use frequently. A quicker method would be to use the Coronet expanding collet chuck.

Lathe Speed

1000 rpm.

Tools

3/8-in (9.6-mm) long and strong bowl gouge
1/4-in (6.3-mm) spindle gouge
Parting tool

Method

Screw the prepared blank to the faceplate, attach it to the lathe and turn down to round. Change the position of the tool rest to across the diameter of the work and mark out with the parting tool. Should the wood-chuck method be used, the center of the block can be cut out immediately, but take care not to strike the faceplate as you break through. If the expanding collet is in use, cut a dovetail recess to receive the collet; when the work is reversed, in removing the center, we shall break through into this recess.

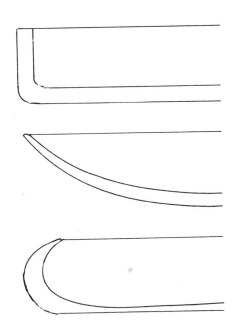

Use the ⅜-in (9.6-mm) gouge to shape the underside, finish as necessary and polish. Remove the faceplate. Either assemble into the wood chuck or insert the expanding collet. In the case of the latter, place a piece of fairly thick paper into the recess before inserting the collet.

Return to the lathe and mark out with the parting tool. Using the gouge, work toward and away from the center to turn the trough. If the collet is in use, carefully remove the center; stop cutting when the tool touches the paper. Clean up and finish the bowl and remove from the chuck.

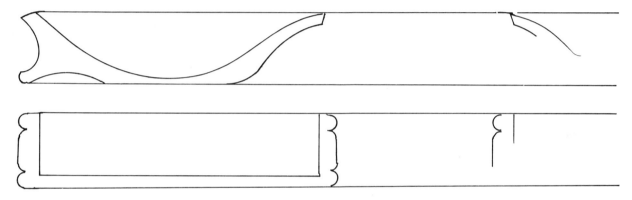

Fig. 24:1.

FIFTH COURSE—CHEESE & CRACKERS

25   Cheese Board

Fig. 25:1. Cheese board with circular tile and glass dome.

Fig. 25:2. Cheese board with in-serted tile.

Design Specification

Many people will prefer to cut the cheese on a plate or ceramic tile and have the cheese covered at all times. The first design incorporates a 6-in (15-cm) circular tile and a glass dome (**25:1-2**).

To hold a variety of cheeses and a cheese knife, a larger board will be needed, in this case made from strips of teak glued together, with a small magnet inserted to hold the knife. Each board needs a crumb rim to prevent cheese crumbs from dropping onto the table.

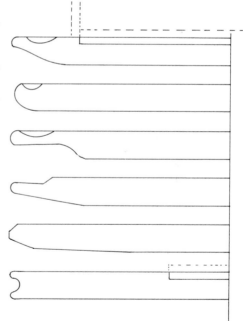

Wood

Sycamore, maple, beech or teak.

Finish

Untreated.

Attachment to the Lathe

Wood-chuck method, or expanding collet chuck.

Lathe Speed

800-1000 rpm.

Tools

⅜-in (9.6-mm) long and strong bowl gouge
¼-in (6.3-mm) spindle gouge
Parting tool

Method

Glue up the strips of teak, cramp up and leave to dry. Use the bandsaw to cut to round and screw up the faceplate. Mount to the lathe, bring up the tool rest and use the ⅜-in (9.6-mm) gouge to turn down to round.

If the wood chuck is to be used, the faceplate can be

Fig. 25:3. Cutting the tile recess with the ⅜-in (9.6-mm) gouge.

removed and the disc inserted. If the expanding collet is available, place the tool rest across the disc and carefully cut a dovetail recess to receive the collet, after first shaping the underside of the board with the gouge. Complete the underside and remove the faceplate. Reassemble on the collet chuck and return to the lathe. Use the gouge to complete the face turning (25:3).

When removed from the lathe, bore a shallow hole to receive the magnet for the knife. If knife blades are available, a matching handle turned between centers would add quality to the job.

Fig. 26:1. Cracker and butter dish in mahogany—knob in laburnum.

26 Cracker and Butter Dish

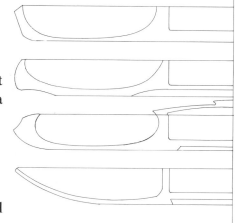

Design Specification

Shallow tray design to hold crackers. Center recess cut to receive a glass insert for butter, the dish itself to have a wooden cover (**26:1**).

Wood

English walnut or black walnut.

Finish

Two coats of white French polish cut back with steel wool.

Attachment to the Lathe

Faceplate/wood chuck.

Lathe Speed

1000 rpm.

Tools

Roughing gouge
⅜-in (9.6-mm) long and strong gouge
Parting tool
Faceplate or screw chuck.

Method

Prepare a wood chuck to receive the dish (or use the expanding collet). First mount the wood on the faceplate and turn to diameter, finishing the edge completely. Remove the faceplate. Place the chuck on the lathe, insert the job, then turn the outside. Reverse and turn the inside, polishing as the job proceeds (26:2).

Remove the completed dish from the chuck. Before removing the chuck, cut a smaller recess in the center to receive the butter-dish lid (26:3). Place the lid block on the screw chuck (26:5). Mount to the lathe and turn the inside of the lid first. Polish and complete.

Remove from the lathe. Reverse and insert in the wood chuck. Now turn down the outside of the lid, also the knob (26:6-8).

Fig. 26:2. Shaping with the ⅜-in (9.6-mm) HSS gouge.

Fig. 26:3. Shaping the recess for the butter dish.

Fig. 26:4. Shaping the cracker ring.

Fig. 26:5. Shaping the butter dish lid.

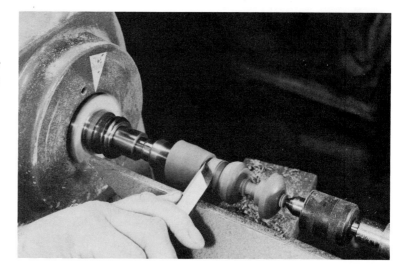

Fig. 26:6. Using the chisel to shape the dish knob (two are made from one piece).

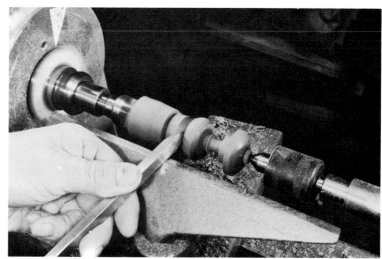

Fig. 26:7. Using the parting tool to cut the tenon.

Fig. 26:8. Squaring the base of the knob with the long corner of the skew chisel.

27 Butter Dish

Design Specification

Design requires smooth, clean lines and a close-fitting
lid (**27:1-2**).

Fig. 27:1-2. Butter dish in walnut.

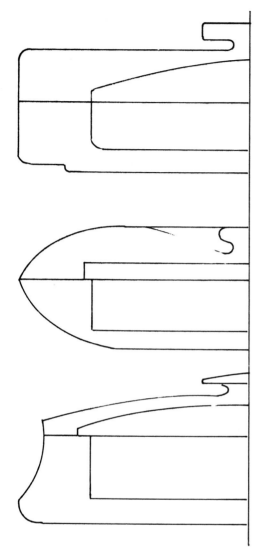

Wood

Cherry, maple or sycamore.

Finish

Hard, acid catalyst finish.

Attachment to the Lathe

Expanding chuck or screw chuck. Wood chuck to mount the lid for turning.

Lathe Speed

1000-1200 rpm.

Tools

⅜-in (9.6-mm) long and strong gouge
¼-in (6.3-mm) spindle gouge
Parting tool

Method

Mount with the ring and expanding universal chuck. Turn the outside of the body (27:3), cutting a dovetail recess to receive the chuck. Complete to finish and polish.

Remove the chuck ring, insert the chuck collet into the dovetail recess. Return to the lathe. Turn out a recess to receive the glass insert. Complete and remove.

Prepare a wood chuck to receive the lid. Turn the lid material to size. Insert the lid disc into the wood chuck and turn the inside of the lid (27:4). Reverse the lid into the chuck and turn the outside of the lid and knob. Polish and complete (27:5).

Fig. 27:3. Shaping the bowl.

Fig. 27:4. Lid shaped inside.

Fig. 27:5. Cutting back the polish with steel wool.

Fig. 28:1. Cracker barrel in elm, with plastic insert.

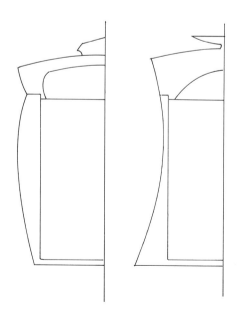

28   Cracker Barrel

Design Specification
To hold approximately a pound of crackers (**28:1**); could have a metal handle added.

Wood
Choose a wood that will not contaminate the crackers in taste or smell.

Finish
Seal with an acid catalyst finish. Cut back each coat to leave an eggshell gloss.

Attachment to the Lathe
Expanding collet chuck and faceplate.

Lathe Speed

800-1000 rpm.

Tools

⅜-in (9.6-mm) long and strong gouge
1-in (2.5-cm) spindle roughing gouge
Parting tool
Spade scraper
⅛-in (3.2-mm) spindle gouge

Method

The Body—Screw the faceplate to the block prepared for the box. Mount to the lathe. Turn down and shape the outside (**28:2**). Complete the dovetail recess. Take from the lathe, remove the ring. Assemble the collet chuck, using the recess. Return to the lathe. Turn the inside of the box (**28:3-5**). Clean up, polish the outside, and remove (**28:6**).

The Lid—Turn the lid with a wood chuck. Mount the disc on a screw chuck. Turn to the correct diameter, then shape the inside of the lid. Clean up and leave unpolished, as with the body. Remove from the chuck. Insert into the wood chuck. Turn the outside of the lid and the knob. Polish and remove from the wood chuck.

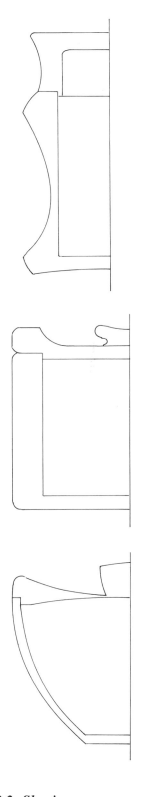

Fig. 28:2. Shaping.

Fig. 28:3. Removing the body waste with the multi-span cutter.

Fig. 28:4. Trimming the side with a scraper.

Fig. 28:5. Checking the barrel liner for fit.

110

Fig. 28:6. Barrel polished.

An alternative method would be to screw a block large enough to provide body, lid and knob to a 3-in (7.5-cm) faceplate. Turn the outside of the barrel, the lid and the knob exactly as turning between centers. Part off the lid. The inside of the lid could be left flat and cleaned up on an abrasive board.

Alternatively, a wood chuck could be prepared and the lid reversed into it to permit the inside to be shaped as with a bowl. Again, if the shape of the knob would permit, the whole could be held in a collet chuck, as long as there is no excessive overhang which may cause the lid to lose centricity when turning.

Using the same tools and method of turning as with a bowl, the inside of the barrel can be turned after the lid has been cut off. When complete, part off and clean up the bottom on an abrasive board.

Another alternative, and to cater to those people who object to crackers stored in wood, is a plastic container inserted into the barrel. A number of these are available, some in clear plastic.

SIXTH COURSE— NUTS

29 Nut Bowl with Waste Rim

Design Specification

Very few nut bowls make provision or have a receptacle for the broken shells. This design incorporates such a feature (**29:1**). A fairly sizeable bowl is required since nuts tend to occupy a great deal of space.

Fig. 29:1. Nut bowl with shell recess, in mahogany.

Wood

Any good hardwood, preferably fairly close-grained.

Finish

Seal with sanding sealer and polish with white French polish.

Attachment to the Lathe

Use the expanding collet chuck and faceplate.

Lathe Speed

1200 rpm.

Tools

⅜-in (9.6-mm) long and strong gouge
Parting tool
½-in (12.7-mm) skew chisel
¼-in (6.3-mm) roundnose spindle gouge

Method

Screw the faceplate to the prepared blank, then assemble it to the lathe. Screw on to the lathe, bring up the tool rest and use the ⅜-in (9.6-mm) long and strong gouge to turn down to round (**29:2**).

With the parting tool, cut a groove to indicate the diameter of the collet, and undercut the dovetail recess for the collet with the long corner of the skew chisel. The chisel will, of course, lie on its side. Remove the waste in the recess with the ¼-in (6.3-mm) roundnose spindle gouge. Begin shaping the underside of the bowl.

Fig. 29:2. Roughing to size.

113

Still using the ⅜-in (9.6-mm) long and strong gouge, work from inside to outside to complete the shaping (**29:3-5**). Clean up and polish (**29:6**). Remove from the lathe, take off the collet and ring. Insert the collet into the prepared recess in the base of the bowl and return to the lathe. Cut a starting point near the rim with the parting tool. Mark out the waste rim.

Again, using the ⅜-in (9.6-mm) long and strong gouge, shape the bowl (**29:7-8**), remembering the golden rule of letting the bevel rub. Cut the waste recess with the same gouge (**29:9**). Make the last few cuts carefully to arrive at a good finish. Clean up and polish.

Fig. 29:3. Shaping the outside—universal chuck recess cut.

Fig. 29:4. Shaping the outside with the ⅜-in (9.6-mm) deep long and strong bowl gouge.

Fig. 29:5. Outside shaping completed (note the smooth finish from the gouge).

Fig. 29:6. Polishing.

Fig. 29:7. Shaping with the ⅜-in (9.6-mm) long and strong gouge.

115

Fig. 29:8. Using the gouge.

Fig. 29:9. Cutting the shell recess.

An alternative method would be to use a faceplate for holding when turning the underside, and a wood chuck to hold the bowl when reversed. Alternatively, a similar recess to that cut for the collet chuck could be used to locate the bowl on a wood block screwed to a faceplate.

30 Nut Dish with Pick Container

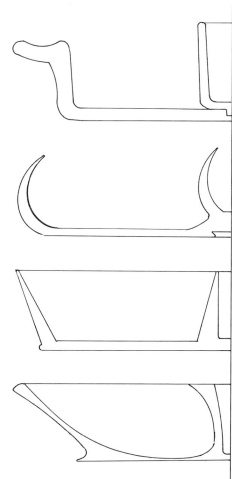

Design Specification

A shallow dish to hold shelled nuts, with a separate holder for picks (**30:1**).

Wood

Walnut or any of the fruit woods.

Finish

Oil.

Attachment to the Lathe

Screw chuck/wood chuck.

Lathe Speed

1200 rpm.

Tools

⅜-in (9.6-mm) long and strong gouge
¼-in (6.3-mm) roundnose spindle gouge
Parting tool
Spade scraper

Method

Use a screw chuck to hold the wood, turn down to round and finish the edge, then transfer to a wood chuck. Alternatively, the block could be mounted base-down on the screw chuck and completed in that position. The screw hole would need to be filled in after completion. A light turning like this could also be held using the glue method.

To turn the dish, first turn to round using the ⅜-in (9.6-mm) long and strong gouge. Mark out with the parting tool and use the ¼-in (6.3-mm) roundnose gouge to remove the waste and shape the dish (**30:2-4**). Sand down and oil.

Fig. 30:2. Turning the underside.

Fig. 30:3. Shaping the dish.

Fig. 30:4. Finishing cut.

The pick holder could also be made using the screw chuck to hold the blank, but in this case the blank was pre-bored and then pushed onto a spigot (pin chuck) held in the body of the expanding collet chuck. This permits the turning of a small tenon on the underside which can be used to locate the holder in the nut dish **(30:5-11)**.

The dish could be further improved with addition of a small handle. This could be carved separately and attached with glue.

Fig. 30:5. Spigot showing pin in inclined.

Fig. 30:6. Spigot attached to collet chuck.

Fig. 30:7. Prebored block in place before turning.

Fig. 30:8. Shaping.

120

Fig. 30:9. Shaping the base.

Fig. 30:10. Cutting the tenon.

Fig. 30:11. Squaring with the long corner of the skew chisel.

Fig. 31:1. Nut bowl with ship's-wheel mechanism.

31 Nut Bowl with Wheel Cracker

Design Specification

A double tray, the inner designed to fit a ship's-wheel cracker mechanism and to receive the broken shells, the outer rim to hold the nuts (**31:1**).

Wood

Teak or another suitable hardwood.

Finish

An easily cleaned finish, using Mazola® or some other good-quality cooking oil.

Attachment to the Lathe

Expanding collet chuck and faceplate. Alternatively, the outside can be turned using a faceplate, then the bowl is reversed into a wood chuck and turned.

Lathe Speed

800 rpm.

Tools

⅜-in (9.6-mm) long and strong gouge
Parting tool
Lip and spur bit
½-in (12.7-mm) skew chisel

Method

Cut a disc roughly to size using the bandsaw or another saw, as available. Screw on a faceplate, and mount to the lathe. Bring up the tool rest and use the ⅜-in (9.6-mm) long and strong gouge to turn down to round. Take the tool rest across the face of the bowl and mark out the expanding collet recess with the parting tool (**31:2**).

Shape the outside with the gouge, keep the bevel of the tool rubbing, removing the waste while simultaneously shaping and surfacing the wood. Bring to a clean finish, scrape, if necessary, either with the standard scraping tools

Fig. 31:2. Expanding collet recess cut with chisel.

or by hand with the lathe stopped. Finish with paper, oil and remove from the lathe.

Reverse the bowl, placing the collet chuck in the prepared recess cut into the underside. Return the assembly to the lathe. Place the tool rest across the bowl and mark out with the parting tool (31:3). Shape with the long and strong gouge (31:4-5) and bring to a final finish as with the outside.

Fig. 31:3. Marked out with the parting tool.

Fig. 31:4. Shaping with the ⅜-in (9.6-mm) long and strong bowl-turning gouge.

Fig. 31:5. Shaping continued.

With a drill chuck placed in the tool rest, use a lip and spur bit to bore a hole in the center to receive the nutcracking mechanism. Remove from the lathe, screw down the ship's-wheel cracker mechanism to complete the work.

Aftercare

Occasionally wipe down with a cloth dipped in a good-quality cooking oil.

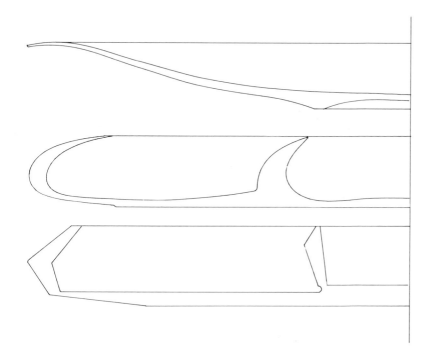

SEVENTH COURSE— COFFEE

32   Cups and Saucers

Fig. 32:1. Cup and saucer in yew.

Design Specification

Simple, easily cleaned curves, cut to thin section (**32:1**). All four pieces will be turned at one time.

Wood

Cherry, clean and free from flaws.

Finish

A two-part acid catalyst mix. Three coats, all cut back and completed in an eggshell finish.

Attachment to the Lathe

Screw-flange chuck with two ⅛-in (3.2-mm) hardboard discs to reduce the length of screw penetration for the cup, and the expanding collet chuck for the saucer.

Lathe Speed

Turn at 1400 rpm, except when boring out the cups with the sawtooth machine cutter, when the speed should be reduced to 900 rpm.

Tools

⅜-in (9.6-mm) long and strong gouge
¼-in and ½-in (6.3-mm and 12.7-mm) standard gouge
Parting tool

Method

The wood will be held by using the screw chuck for the cup and the expanding collet chuck for the saucer. The collet recess will be a feature of the design in the case of the saucer.

Fig. 32:2. Disc turned on the screw chuck and marked out.

Making the Saucer—Mount the disc of wood on the screw chuck. Mark out with pencil and parting tool (**32:2-3**). With the ½-in or ¼-in (12.7-mm or 6.3-mm) gouge, remove waste and accurately cut to shape and size (**32:4**). Cut the dovetailed recess to receive the chuck (**32:5**). Finish by cutting back, burnishing and finally polishing.

Remove from the screw chuck and remount, using the dovetailed recess. Mark out with pencil and parting tool and shape with the gouge (**32:6-7**). Take care to run to a thin edge and section. Repeat with all four saucers.

Fig. 32:3. Marking out with the parting tool.

Fig. 32:4. Shaping the underside of the saucer with the ¼-in (6.3-mm) gouge.

Fig. 32:5. Cutting the dovetail recess.

Fig. 32:6. Plate reversed; expanding collet inserted into the dovetail recess.

Fig. 32:7. Shaping with the gouge.

Turning the Cup—Mount the rough block, using a screw chuck (**32:8**). Turn to round, mark out with pencil and parting tool (**32:9**) and shape the cup using the ¼-in or ⅜-in (6.3-mm or 9.6-mm) gouge. Finish the outside of the cup up to the pre-polishing stage (**32:10-11**). Cut a recess near the edge with the parting tool and bore to depth at the center with either the ¼-in (6.3-mm) standard gouge or a sawtooth cutter (**32:12**).

Remove the waste and shape the cup inside, using either a ⅜-in (9.6-mm) bowl-turning gouge or a scraper with an egg-shaped nose. Bring to a final finish and polish. Clear the waste material at the base. Part off the cup.

Fig. 32:8. Block mounted on the screw chuck, rough-turned and marked out.

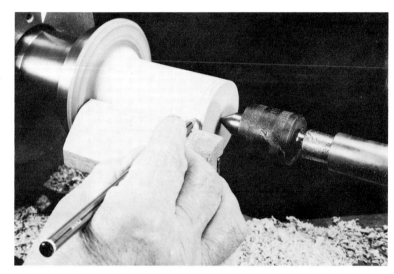

Fig. 32:9. Marking out with the narrow parting tool.

Fig. 32:10. Planing to size and shape with the skew chisel.

Fig. 32:11. Squaring the end with the long corner of the skew chisel.

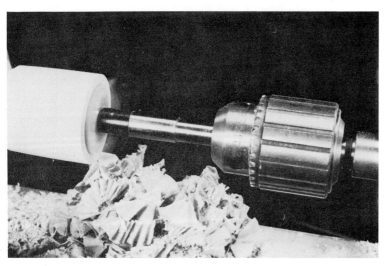

Fig. 32:12. Boring with the sawtooth cutter.

Fig. 32:13. Removing the waste at the base with the ¼-in (6.3-mm) spindle gouge.

Fig. 32:14. Parting off the cup.

Making the Handles—Select cherry to match the cups. Cut a small section and bore the finger hole with a ¾-in (19-mm) forstner bit or other suitable machine bit. Shape with the coping saw or jigsaw, if available. Complete shaping with the spokeshave. Sand, seal and polish. Glue up, using an epoxy resin glue.

Fig. 33:1. Sugar bowl in English walnut.

33 Sugar Bowl

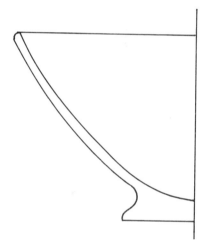

Design Specification
Simple shape with size based on an average family need (**33:1**).

Wood
Burma teak.

Finish
Two-part acid catalyst mix. Three coats, cut back with steel wool and left an eggshell finish.

Attachment to the Lathe
Expanding collet chuck and ring with dovetail recess.

Lathe Speed
Turn at 1200-1400 rpm.

Tools
⅜-in (9.6-mm) long and strong gouge
Parting tool
¼-in (6.3-mm) spindle gouge

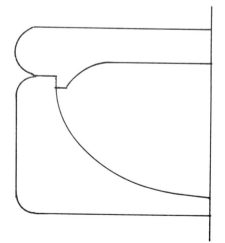

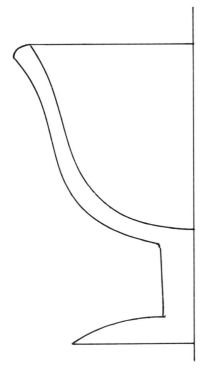

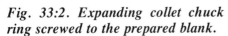

Method

Screw the ring to the sawn block and use the expanding collet chuck to attach to the lathe (**33:2-3**). Turn the outside first, cutting a recess to receive the chuck when the work is reversed.

Turning the Bowl—Turn to round. Mark out with the parting tool. Cut the dovetail recess sized to suit the smaller expanding collet (**33:4**). Use the deep gouge to shape the outside of the bowl, base and pedestal (**33:5**). Complete the outside turning.

Reverse the turning, remove the mounting ring and place the expanding collet in position to firmly grip the block. Reassemble to the lathe. Mark out with parting tool and ¼-in (6.3-mm) gouge to indicate internal diameter and the depth of the bowl. Use the ⅜-in (9.6-mm) deep long and strong gouge to remove the waste and complete the shape. A scraping chisel can be used to obtain a finer finish (**33:6**). Bring to a finish, polish and remove the completed bowl.

Fig. 33:2. Expanding collet chuck ring screwed to the prepared blank.

Fig. 33:3. Expanding collet chuck in place, screwed up tightly with "C" spanners.

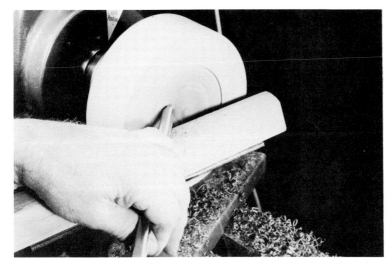

Fig. 33:4. Cutting the dovetail recess to receive the chuck when reversed.

Fig. 33:5. Shaping the outside.

Fig. 33:6. Cleaning up with the scraper.

EIGHTH COURSE— PETIT FOURS

34 Petit Fours Dish

Design Specification

Tray to hold various brands of after-dinner mints or petit fours (**34:1**).

Fig. 34:1. Petit fours dish in Circassian walnut.

Wood

As available, or to match or contrast with existing equipment.

Finish

Two coats of hard finish cut back with steel wool to an eggshell finish.

Attachment to the Lathe

Expanding collet chuck.

Lathe Speed

1200-1400 rpm.

Tools

Parting tool
⅜-in (9.6-mm) long and strong gouge
Spade scraper

Method

Prepare and mount the wood on a faceplate. Mark out the collet recess and the trough with the parting tool (**34:2**). Accurately cut the dovetail recess with the long corner of the skew chisel. Use the gouge to remove the waste and shape the dish (**34:3-4**).

Final squaring will need to be done with the spade chisel. Scrape carefully, trailing the chisel to produce a shaving. Clean up and polish.

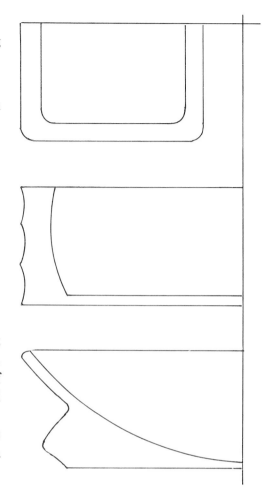

Fig. 34:2. Marking out a recess.

Remove from the lathe, insert the collet chuck and tighten it down quite firmly (**34:5-6**). Return the job to the lathe and once again mark out the underside of the dish.

Fig. 34:3. Shaping with the gouge.

Fig. 34:4.Rounding the edge with the gouge.

Fig. 34:5. Inserting the chuck.

Turn, shape and remove the center section completely up to the face of the collet (**34:7-8**). Clean up, seal and polish.

Remove from the lathe, and unscrew the expanding collet to complete the work.

Fig. 34:6. *Tightening the chuck.*

Fig. 34:7. *Removing the center waste.*

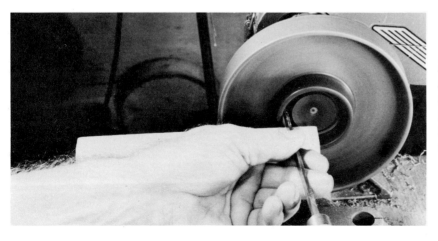

Fig. 34:8. *Parting up to the face of the collet (a disc of white paper placed inside the recess before the chuck is assembled will help).*

FOR THE KITCHEN

35   Steak Tenderizer

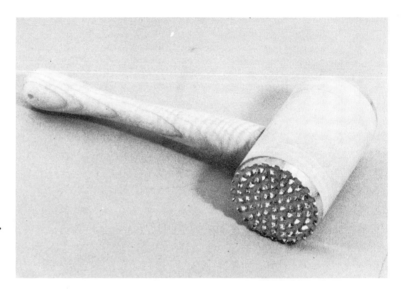

Fig. 35:1.

Design Specification

A clean design is needed, with size partly dictated by the size of the metal inserts (**35:1**). Metal inserts need not be used, but the ends will have to be carefully cut with saw and chisel to produce the tenderizing points.

Wood

Beech, maple or sycamore with handle of ash or hickory. Alternatively, the mallet could be made in one piece, using beech throughout.

Finish

As left from tools.

Attachment to the Lathe

Wood is assembled between the normal centers, although the square-sectioned billets could be placed without preparation into the Coronet cone chucks.

Lathe Speed

1400 rpm.

Tools

¾-in (19-mm) standard roughing gouge
1-in (2.5-cm) skew chisel
Parting tool
¼-in (6.3-mm) roundnose spindle gouge

Method

Rough down with the ¾-in (19-mm) deep gouge and plane to perfection with the 1-in (2.5-cm) skew chisel. Mark out with pencil and parting tool. Use the roundnose gouge to shape the mallet head, and the long corner of the skew chisel to square the ends, completing the head (**35:2**).

Turn the handle in the same way, forming a tenon at one end. Use the skew chisel to shape and finish. Remove from the lathe.

Accurately mark out the head and bore the center to receive the tenon of the handle. Bore both ends and glue the metal inserts in place with an epoxy resin glue.

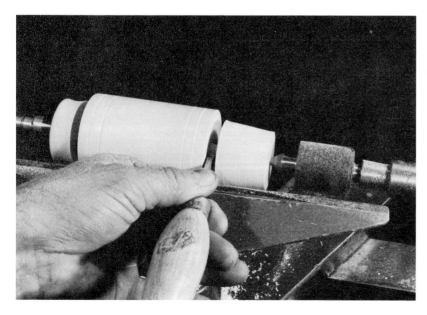

Fig. 35:2. Parting off the head.

Fig. 36:1

36 Mortar and Pestle

Design Specification

Attention must be paid to the restricted function of this particular piece of equipment. The curve of the pestle end must match the curvature of the mortar. The pestle must be a comfortable fit in the hand with the mortar firmly placed on the tabletop (**36:1**).

Wood

Sycamore, maple or beech.

Finish

Left from the tool.

Attachment to the Lathe

Use the expanding collet chuck for the mortar. Turn the pestle between centers or use the cone centers.

Alternatively, the screw chuck or a faceplate could be used, parting off the mortar to avoid leaving screw holes in the base.

Lathe Speed

1200 rpm.

Tools

⅜-in (9.6-mm) long and strong gouge
¾-in (19-mm) standard roughing gouge
Parting tool
¼-in (6.3-mm) roundnose gouge

Method

For the mortar, follow the same procedure as when cutting a bowl; the pestle will also be a piece of simple spindle turning.

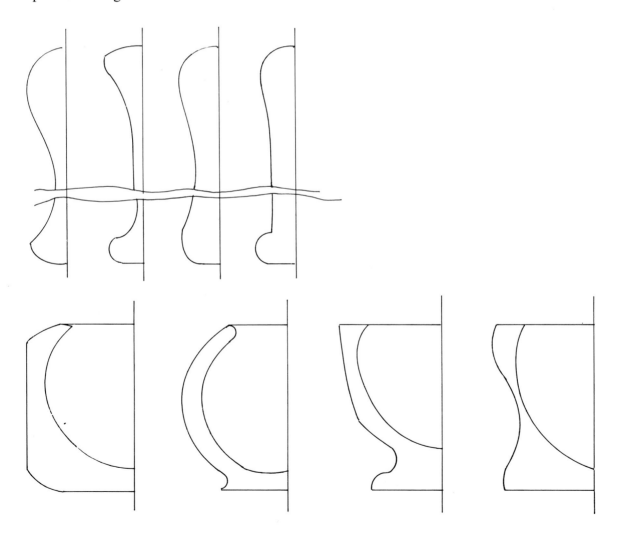

Fig. 37:1. Nutmeg grinder in English yew.

37   Nutmeg Grinder

Design Specification
This is a kitchen utensil and the design must have clean lines and be easy to take apart for cleaning (**37:1**).

Wood
Any wood having a strong smell should be avoided. Once again, the garden woods, particularly from the fruit trees, will be suitable, although the sample shown was made in English Yew.

Finish
A washable finish that will not deteriorate in use is required.

Attachment to the Lathe
This small project can be held quite securely on a

screw chuck. The end must be cut square and, if at all possible, slightly concave to provide a tight fit against the face of the chuck. Alternatively, it can be prepared between centers for final mounting in the collar chuck.

Lathe Speed

1400 rpm for turning.
1000 rpm when drilling.

Tools

Screw chuck or collar chuck. If the collar chuck is used, a driving fork and running centers will be needed to pre-turn the blank between centers. A 1-in (2.5-cm) spindle gouge or ¾-in (19-mm) deep standard gouge for roughing to size; a 1-in (2.5-cm) skew chisel for planing; a ½-in (12.7-mm) skew chisel for shaping; a ¼-in (6.3-mm) roundnose gouge for shaping; parting tools; sawtooth cutters or flatbits or similar for boring; a ¼-in (6.3-mm) wood drill. A tailstock drill chuck with arbor to suit the lathe.

Method

Prepare the block, square off one end and slightly in-curve. Mark the center and bore a small hole to receive the screw of the chuck.

Place the screw chuck into position on the headstock and wind on the blank. Set the tee rest slightly above center and as close to the work as possible. Use a ¾-in (19-mm) deep roughing gouge to quickly turn down to round (37:2). Plane down to size with the 1-in (2.5-cm) skew chisel. Mark

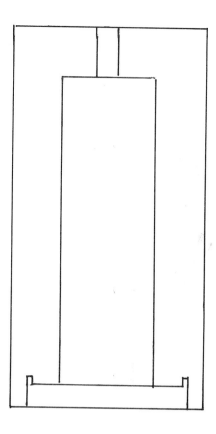

Fig. 37:2. Turned to round and marked out.

145

out as necessary with pencil and parting tool, and use both chisel and gouge to shape the grinder (**37:3**).

Clean up and polish the outside. Fit the tailstock chuck in place of the running center, secure the 1¾-in (4.5-cm) sawtooth cutter in the chuck and bore to a depth of ¼-in (6.3-mm) (**37:4**).

Replace the 1¾-in (4.5-cm) cutter with the 1-in (2.5-cm) and bore out the body to a depth of 3 in (7.5 cm) (**37:5**). Remove this bit and replace with a ¼-in (6.3-mm) wood drill. Clean up the inside with sandpaper, if necessary.

Place the tee rest across the base of the grinder and, with the ⅛-in (3.2-cm) parting tool, cut a small groove inside the 1¾-in (4.5-cm) recess to a depth of ³⁄₁₆ in (5 mm). This recess will receive the upturned rim of the grinder cutter (**37:6**).

Fig. 37:3. Shaping with the skew chisel.

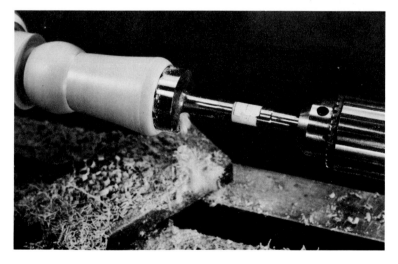

Fig. 37:4. Boring with the sawtooth cutter.

Alternative Method of Boring Out the Body—If boring tools are not available, place the tool rest across the end of the grinder and use a parting tool to mark up the 1¾-in (4.5-cm) diameter, making a groove which will serve as a starting point for the gouge. Now use the ¼-in (6.3-mm) roundnose gouge to remove and shape the inside of the body. Final clearance of the bottom inside may need the use of a small spade scraper. Cut the little recess as previously.

Replace the tee rest and prepare to part off, but first make sure that the finish is satisfactory. Widen the parting-off groove to make room for the safe insertion of the

½-in (12.7-cm) skew chisel for final parting off to a good smoooth finish **(37:7)**.

To Insert the Grinder Mechanism—Push the spinner into the body through the ¼-in (6.3-mm) hole, and screw on the locking arm and nut. This will place the spring under tension. Use two countersunk brass head screws to secure the cutter plate in the base of the body. The grinder is now ready for use. Place a nutmeg into the body, slide the closure plate in place and proceed to make your rice pudding or eggnog.

Fig. 37:7. Parting off with the ½-in (12.7-mm) skew chisel.

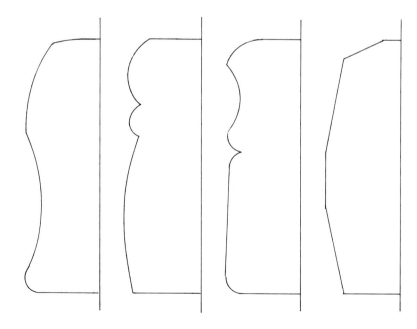

Fig. 38:1.

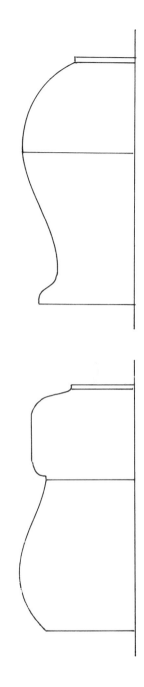

38 Coffee Grinder

Design Specification
The type of mechanism chosen will, to a certain extent, place limitations on the design. Certainly, the grinder must stand on a firm base; at the same time, a secure hold for the left hand must be provided **(38:1)**.

Wood
Any good hardwood but, once again, attention must be paid to the selection of wood without strong odor or anything which may affect the taste of the coffee.

Finish
A hard sealer, but the final decision will depend on the wood selected.

Attachment to the Lathe

This is a two-part turning; the top piece will best be held in the expanding collet chuck, the base in this chuck or on a screw chuck. Alternatively, the small faceplate can be pressed into use, but the ⅛-in (3.2-mm) recess to accommodate the strap will need to be cut entirely by hand.

Lathe Speed

1200 rpm.

Tools

½-in and 1-in (12.7-mm and 2.5-cm) skew chisels
Parting tool
¼-in (6.3-mm) spindle gouge
⅜-in (9.6-mm) long and strong bowl gouge
1⅝-in and 2¼-in (4- and 5.7-cm) sawtooth cutters
Tailstock drill chuck

Method

Turning the Base—Screw the block to the screw chuck, turn to round, and shape the outside. Bring the tool rest across the face, mark out with parting tool and spindle gouge as with other bowls. Remove the waste and shape the inside of the base. Use the parting tool to recess the edge to receive the top. Finish as necessary and remove from the lathe (**38:3-5**).

Turning the Top—Again, use the screw chuck to hold the block. Turn to round and shape (**38:6**). Prepare a recess

Fig. 38:2. Checking the bowl for fit.

150

Fig. 38:3. Beginning to shape the base.

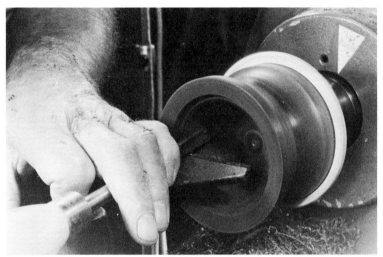

Fig. 38:4. Deep cutting with the ⅜-in (9.6-mm) HSS gouge.

Fig. 38:5. Shaping the outside.

Fig. 38:6. Shaping the top.

Fig. 38:7. Cutting the lip with the skew chisel.

Fig. 38:8. Squaring the lip with the heel of the skew chisel.

to receive the expanding collet chuck, unscrew the block from the screw chuck and reassemble to the collet. (Place a thick piece of paper in the bottom of the recess before reassembly.)

Use the parting tool to cut the small step in the underside of the top so that the top will be a good fit in the base (**38:7-8**). Secure a 2¼-in (5.7-cm) sawtooth cutter in the tailstock chuck and bore a hole to a depth of ½ in (12.7 mm). Replace the 2¼-in (5.7-cm) cutter with a 1⅝-in (4-cm) and bore to exactly 1 in (2.5 cm) of depth. This hole will just break through into the expanding collet recess indicated by the paper which also provides a protection for the sawtooth cutter. (Alternatively, these recesses which house the body of the grinder can be cut with gouge and parting tool.) Clean up and polish as necessary, then remove from the lathe and unscrew the collet chuck.

To Assemble (**38:9-16**)—Push the metal body into the underside of the top and secure with two roundhead brass screws. Insert the body collar from the top into the 1⅝-in (4-cm) recess, place the bracket in position over the collar and screw down with four roundhead brass screws.

The brass bowl can now be fitted over the top and screwed down firmly with three roundhead brass screws. Push the grinder through the top from underneath. Screw on the actuating handle and think about drinking some excellent coffee.

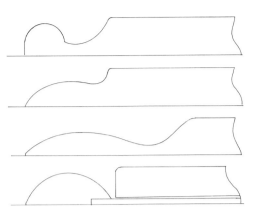

Fig. 38:9. Components prior to assembly.

153

Fig. 38:10. Inserting the body sleeve.

Fig. 38:11. Body positioned in sleeve.

Fig. 38:12. Body secured with screws.

Fig. 38:13. Bracket screwed in place.

Fig. 38:14. Brass bowl secured.

Fig. 38:15. Actuating nut screwed in.

155

Fig. 38:16. Handle screwed on.

Note—There are a number of different designs for coffee grinders which may necessitate slight changes in size and internal design. You should check all details before cutting wood blanks.

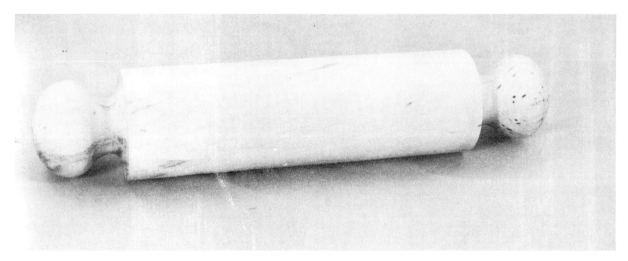

Fig. 39:1.

39 Rolling Pin

Design Specification
A simple design with good handgrips for easy rolling (39:1).

Wood
Sycamore or maple. The wood must be a very close-grained hardwood.

Finish
As left by the cutting tools.

Attachment to the Lathe
Lathe centers or core centers.

Lathe Speed
1400 rpm.

Tools
¾-in (19-mm) roughing gouge or 1-in (2.5-cm) ground
    square across
Spindle gouge
1-in (2.5-cm) skew chisel
½-in (12.7-mm) roundnose spindle gouge
Parting tool

Method

Place the prepared blank between centers, i.e., between the driving fork and the running center. Alternatively, the Coronet cone centers can be brought into use; these will obviate the need to prepare the ends of the wood to receive the centers.

Rough to round with the ¾-in (19-mm) gouge and plane carefully with the 1-in (2.5-cm) skew chisel to the exact diameter. Mark out with the parting tool. Carefully shape the handles with gouge and chisel (**39:2**). Finish with paper if necessary; finally part off with the parting tool or skew chisel.

An alternative design might provide running handles mounted on dowel pin through the rolling pin.

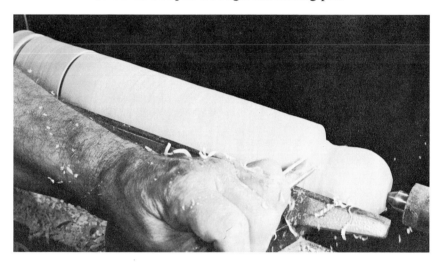

Fig. 39:2. Shaping with the gouge.

Fig. 40:1.

40 Potato Masher

Design Specification
Simple, clean lines with no crevices or decoration that can become filled with mashed food (**40:1**).

Wood
Sycamore, beech or maple, or any close-grained hardwood that will not be affected by constant washing and will not contaminate the food.

Finish
Leave from the tools.

Lathe Speed
1400 rpm.

Attachment to the Lathe
Between centers, using a driving fork and running center.

Tools
¾-in (19-mm) standard gouge
½-in and 1-in (12.7-mm and 2.5-cm) skew chisels
Parting tool
¼-in (6.3-mm) roundnose spindle gouge

Method

Place between centers, bring up the tee rest and set slightly above the height of centers. Rough down to round with the ¾-in (19-mm) deep standard gouge. Plane to size with the 1-in (2.5-cm) skew chisel. Remember to start the cut just in from the end. Reverse direction of movement of the chisel to plane the other end (**40:2-5**).

Mark out with the parting tool. Use the roughing gouge to cut the basic shape. Moving the gouge in the opposite direction so that you work from large diameter to small, use the skew chisel to fine up the curves (**40:6-9**).

The corners can be slightly rolled over with the ¼-in (6.3-mm) roundnose gouge, or the ½-in (12.7-mm) skew chisel can be used. The base must be squared with the long corner of the 1-in (2.5-cm) skew chisel (**40:10**). Slightly incurve the bottom of the masher, using the ¼-in (6.3-mm) roundnose gouge, starting from a tiny groove near the edge (**40:11**).

Carefully part off after finishing, as necessary (**40:12**).

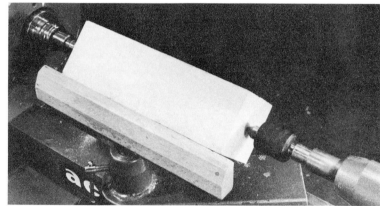

Fig. 40:2. Block mounted between centers.

Fig. 40:3. Roughing to round with the ¾-in (19-mm) deep standard gouge.

160

Fig. 40:4. Planing with the 1-in (2.5-cm) skew chisel.

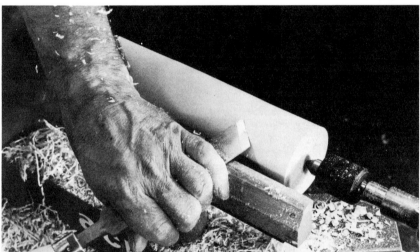

Fig. 40:5. Planing with the skew chisel, reverse direction.

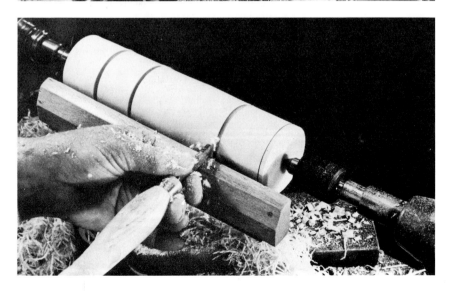

Fig. 40:6. Marking out with the parting tool.

161

Fig. 40:7. Roughing to shape with the roundnose gouge.

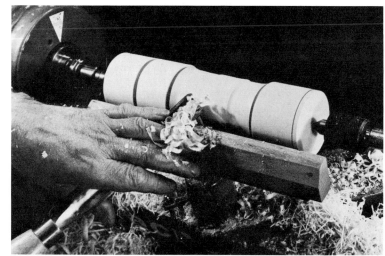

Fig. 40:8. Roughing to shape, reverse direction.

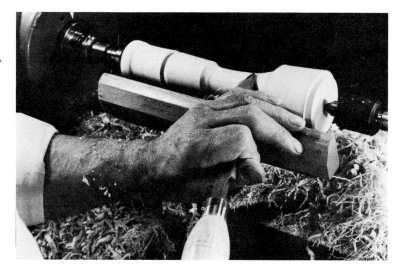

Fig. 40:9. Fining with the skew chisel.

162

Fig. 40:10. Squaring with the long corner of the skew chisel.

Fig. 40:11. Using the ¼-in (6.3-mm) gouge to incurve the base.

Fig. 40:12. Parting off.

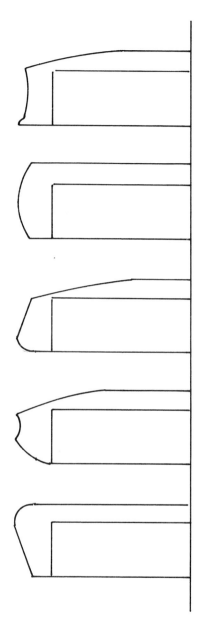

Fig. 41:1

FOR BREAKFAST

41 Marmalade or Jampot Top

Design Specification

A design to enable the ordinary jam jar to be used on the table. The metal lid of the standard jar is to be glued into the wooden top. It can be transferred from jar to jar. This design can be used for other jars, for example, pickle jars, onion jars, etc. (**41:1**).

Wood
Any colorful wood.

Finish
Two coats of white French polish or sanding sealer.

Attachment to the Lathe
Screw chuck.
Squeeze chuck.
Jubilee clip chuck.

Lathe Speed
1200-1400 rpm.

Tools
Squeeze chuck or clip chuck
¼-in (6.3-mm) spindle gouge
Parting tool

Method
Attach the prepared disc to the screw chuck, placing a disc of ⅛-in (3.2-mm) hardboard between the chuck and the wood. Shape the outside of the top; clean up. Polish and

Fig. 41:2. Wood attached to glue chuck and turned to round.

remove from the chuck. Insert into the squeeze chuck or the Jubilee clip chuck. With the parting tool, mark out the recess to receive the pot lid. Use the ¼-in (6.3-mm) gouge to remove the waste. Fit and glue the metal lid in place—use an epoxy resin for this. Remove from the chuck.

Alternatively, if the top of the job is to be flat, the glue chuck can be used to hold the prepared wood. The work can be turned to size and the recess for the lid cut with the parting tool and ¼-in (6.3-mm) spindle gouge (41:2-6).

A simple wood chuck could also be used to receive blanks turned on the glue chuck.

Fig. 41:3. Sizing the inside with calipers.

Fig. 41:4. Checking for fit.

Fig. 41:5. Bottle lid glued in place; glass bottle screwed home.

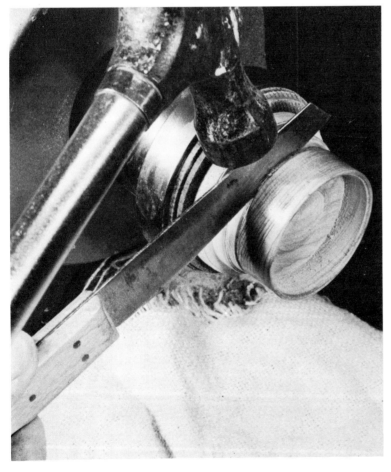

Fig. 41:6. Removing lid with knife and hammer.

167

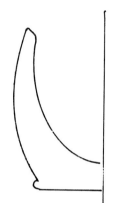

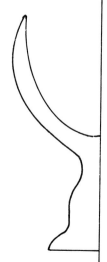

42   Egg Cups

Design Specification

Uncomplicated design is needed to make cleaning easy **(42:1)**.

Wood

Beech or sycamore.

Finish

Hard catalyst finish—three coats cut back with steel wool.

Attachment to the Lathe

Screw chuck.

Lathe Speed

1400 rpm.

Tools

Parting tool
¼-in (6.3-mm) gouge
Egg-shaped scraping chisel

Method

One-setting turning. Turn to round. Mark out and shape the outside. To cut the inside, mark out with parting tool and ¼-in (6.3-mm) gouge. Use gouge to remove waste and shape. Improve the inside if necessary with the scraping chisel (**42:2-7**).

Clean up and polish.

Fig. 42:2. Blank screwed to the screw chuck, turned to round and marked out. (Note the new Coronet tool rest.)

Fig. 42:3. Marking out with the parting tool.

Fig. 42:4. Marking the depth with the round ⅜-in (9.6-mm) gouge.

Fig. 42:5. Shaping the bowl with the ¼-in (6.3-mm) gouge.

Fig. 42:6. Shaping the outside with the gouge.

Fig. 42:7. Fining with the skew chisel.

Appendix A

Spindle gouges

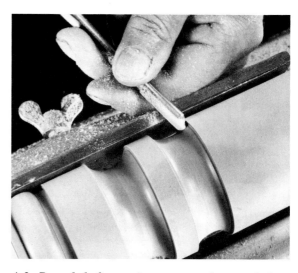

A:3. Rounded, for cutting coves and general shaping between centers; can also be used for bowl work because its corners are ground back (see below).

A:1. Standard roughing gouge—used to bring wood down to round, for general roughing down and sizing.

A:4. Using the gouge for inside bowl work.

A:2. Deep standard gouge—used to bring wood quickly to round, for general roughing down and sizing.

A:5. Using the gouge for turning the outside of a bowl.

172

Skew chisel

Parting tool

A:6. *Planing wood with the skew chisel; also used for finishing.*

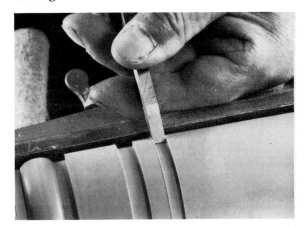

A:9. *Parting off; also used for marking out and beading.*

A:7. *Squaring the end with the long corner of the skew chisel.*

A:10. *Sizing with the parting tool.*

A:8. *Rounding over. Also for beading, curving and tapering.*

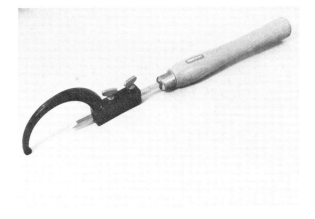

A:11. *Parting tool with the sizing tool, used for marking out.*

Bowl gouge

A:12. Deep long and strong bowl-turning gouge, ground square across.

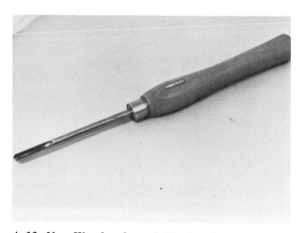

A:13. New Woodcraft steel-alloy bowl gouge. Small bowl gouges are used for inside and outside work on the faceplate or screw chuck, and for shaped spindle work.

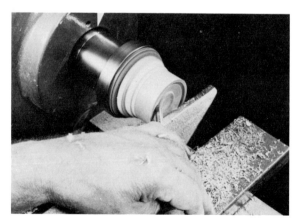

A:14. Mini-bowl turning.

Other useful tools

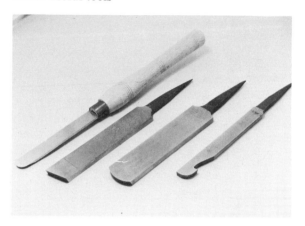

A:15. Various scraping chisels.

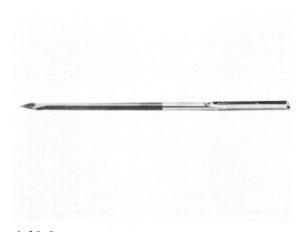

A:16. Lamp standard boring auger.

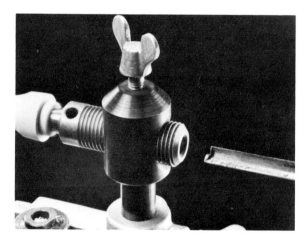

A:17. Long hole boring with the Ridgway lamp standard auger.

174

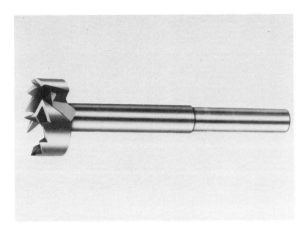

A:18. Sawtooth cutter.

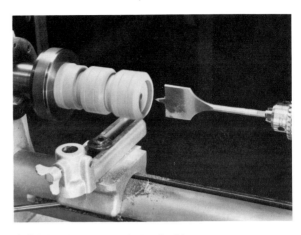

A:21. Boring out with the flatbit.

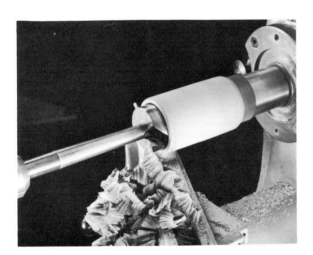

A:19. Boring a pepper mill with the sawtooth cutter.

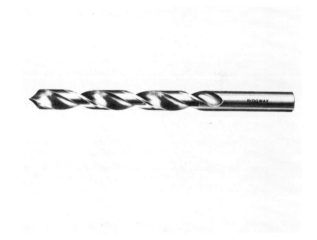

A:22. Wood drill.

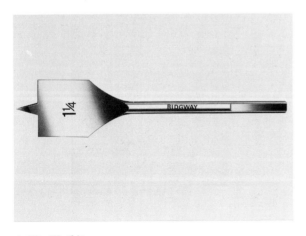

A:20. Flatbit.

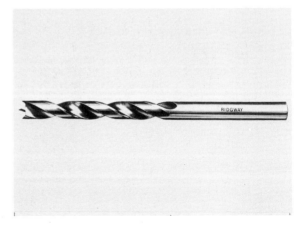

A:23. Lip and spur drill.

Appendix B

Holding Wood for Turning
Between centers

There are a number of methods in use and a wide range of equipment from which to select the correct accessories for the particular turning.

Straight-forward turning between centers (**B:1**) requires a *driving fork* placed in the headstock and a *dead center* located in the tailstock, which can be moved to any position along the lathe bed and adjusted to hold the wood securely. There are a number of variations in both driving centers and tailstock-mounted centers (**B:2-7**).

B:4. Smallest 2-chisel type.

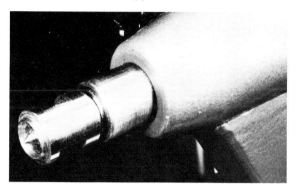

B:5. Cup center.

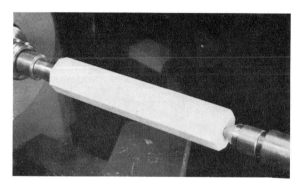

B:1. Wood mounted between centers.

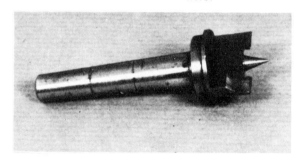

B:2. Prong center, 2-chisel type.

B:6. Prong center, 4-chisel type.

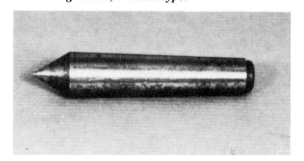

B:3. Solid center.

B:7. Revolving (or running) center.

176

One of the latest methods is to use the *cone drive* (**B:8-10**). Square or round stock can be accommodated as well as work in halves and quarters, which can be used in conjunction with the *normal dead* or *running center*.

Alternatively, and vital with halves or quarters, a *running cone* can be used in the tailstock. The cone drive permits profile turning by placing a turned half or quarter with the unturned half or quarters. The cone centers for the headstock are available with taper to suit the lathe, or are threaded to screw to the headstock mandrel (**B:11**).

A center used when long-hole boring to reverse the wood after boring halfway is the *center and counterboring tool* (**B:12**). It can also be used as a counterboring tool, boring a hole 1 in (25 mm) in diameter.

A mandrel which uses the headstock taper and a running center in the tailstock is ideal, particularly in the making of wheels (**B:13**) and other articles which are pre-bored. Five sizes are available.

B:10. *Running cone.*

B:11. *Morse tapers screw-threaded to receive cones.*

B:8. *Revolving center with 3 inserts.*

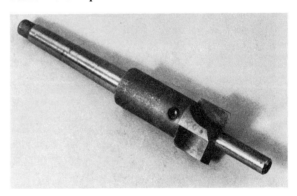

B:12. *Counterboring tool.*

B:9. *Coronet cone centers.*

B:13. *Mandrel (with wood bored and assembled).*

Holding wood on the lathe headstock

Faceplates (**B:14-15**) are available in several sizes from 3 to 14 in (7.5 to 35 cm), threaded either left or right hand depending on the type of lathe. The plates are bored and countersunk to receive screws which hold the turned wood. Large or small pieces can be securely held, but with the disadvantage of holes remaining in the base of the finished work.

B:14. Faceplate.

B:15. Faceplate in use.

B:16. Coronet screw chucks.

A *screw chuck* (**B:16-17**) is a faceplate with a center screw; the best type has a facility for changing the screw for both length and gauge. Available in a number of sizes, starting from 1¼ in (3.2 cm) diameter, it is ideal for holding small work for boxes, egg cups and such work. A number of Universal chucks incorporate a screw-chuck facility.

The *cup chuck* (**B:18-19**) is a simple hollow chuck tapered to hold small pieces of wood.

The *collar chuck* (**B:20-22**) was designed to hold wood without the use of screws. The pre-turned wood is secured to a back plate with a collar, which bears against a flange cut at the end of the wood. The wood cannot break loose. Ideal for egg cups, napkin rings, vases and other small-diameter work.

B:17. Screw chuck with hardboard discs.

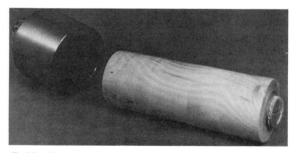

B:18. Cup chuck.

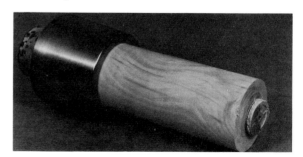

B:19. Cup chuck in use.

178

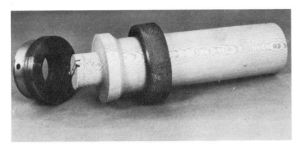

B:20. Collar chuck.

B:21. Collar chuck in use (sample of prepared wood below).

B:22. Collar chucks: (a) Child coil, (b) Six in one, (c) Coronet.

The *Child coil chuck* and the *six-in-one chuck* (**B:22**) have a collar which gives greater capacity for the wood—the Child up to 3½-in (9-cm) diameter, the six-in-one up to 2½ in (6.3 cm) in diameter, and the Coronet collet chuck up to 1⅜ in (3.5 cm).

With the *coil chuck* (**B:23-24**), a coil spring fitting into a pre-cut groove in the wood holds the wood securely. The wood is inserted from the front, thus capacity is only limited by the center height of the lathe centers.

The *collet chuck* (**B:25-26**) is for holding round or square stock up to 1 in (2.5 cm) in diameter. Three sizes of collet are provided with this chuck. Ideal for small knobs and slender work of all kinds.

The *expanding collet chuck* (**B:27-28**) (Six-in-one chuck) is the ideal chuck for bowl turning. It consists of a collar chuck fitted with an expander which actuates an expanding four-jaw collet. The collets move into a pre-cut, dovetailed recess in the underside of a bowl or box to hold it securely. Several sizes of collet are available. With one expanding collet chuck, a range of sizes of recessed plates can be bought which can be used instead of the normal faceplate.

B:23. Child coil chuck, with wood prepared for assembly.

B:24. Child coil chuck, wood in position.

B:25. Collet chuck.

B:26. Coronet collet chuck, with expanding jaws fitted.

B:27. Coronet expanding collet.

B:28. Small, medium, and large expanding collets.

The back plate of the expanding chuck (Six-in-one) can also be used as a faceplate (**B:29**), and also as a *spigot chuck* (**B:30**), using the internal screw thread.

B:29. Six-in-one backplate used as faceplate.

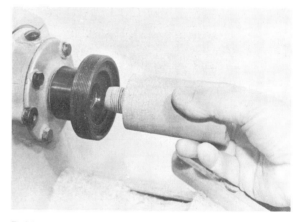

B:30. Six-in-one body used as spigot chuck.

A *split ring* permits the holding of pre-turned wood (**B:31-33**). The collar fits into a groove and is held in place by screwing down on the chuck collar. By inserting the split ring and a center plate, fitted with a center screw, the expanding collet chuck converts to a screw chuck (**B:34**).

The *peppermill chuck, spigot or pin mandrel* (**B:35**) is designed to hold pre-bored wood in the making of pepper and salt mills and other small hollow ware. The wood is securely held by the action of a steel pin riding up an inclined keyway in the chuck cylinder.

B:31. Collar chuck with split ring and prepared wood (1).

B:32. Collar chuck in recess, wood through the ring (2).

B:33. Chuck and wood in place (3).

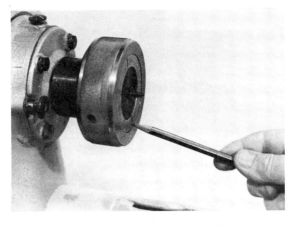

B:34. Six-in-one set up as screw chuck.

B:35. Coronet pin mandrels.

181

Appendix C

Sharpening the Tools

Before considering the action of cutting tools on the lathe, we ought to look at wood cutting in general, in order to assess the needs. The best approach is to look at planing. To plane wood correctly, we must first sharpen the cutting iron. This is carried out on an oilstone, in order to arrive at a very fine, hairline cutting edge. The cap iron is then assembled to the cutter and set $1/16$ in (1.6 mm) from the cutting edge. The complete cutting unit is then carefully returned to the plane, the frog of which has been adjusted to give the correct mouth size. By carefully adjusting the cutting unit to show a hairline cutting edge below the sole of the plane, planing can commence.

The action of planing comprising the cutting and lifting of the shaving. The smaller the lift (controlled by the mouth size), the better the surface will be, but the final finish is obtained by the sole of the plane burnishing the wood after the point of cut. The better the surface finish of the sole, the finer the finish on the wood will be.

With all cutting tools, there is a need to imitate the planing process. We must, therefore, not only produce a perfectly sharp tool, but the quality of the bevel in the case of chisels and gouges must also be of the highest.

The tools of the woodturner must be regarded as planes. Their action will be exactly similar. They won't have a cap iron to turn and break the shaving, but the angle of the bevel will achieve this in the case of the chisel, and the inside curve in the case of the gouge. All the turning tools are sharpened on the ground bevel so that the bevel acts as the sole and burnishes the wood after the point of cut.

For sharpening, a medium-grit India stone, $6 \times 2 \times 1$ in ($15 \times 5 \times 2.5$ cm) will suffice, but if an extremely fine finish is required, one which will not require additional treatment, use a Hard Arkansas stone of the same size. The gouge should be ground at 40°, the bevel should follow the curve of the tool and, when using the ordinary flat oilstone, a rocking motion from side to side must be given to the tool as it is passed backwards and forwards across the stone. A wire

edge will eventually appear on the inside of the gouge and, when this extends along the whole edge, it should be removed with an oilstone slip. This is probably best done by holding against the bench and keeping the slip flat in the groove of the gouge. Do not in any way round over towards the cutting edge.

C:1. Sharpening the gouge.

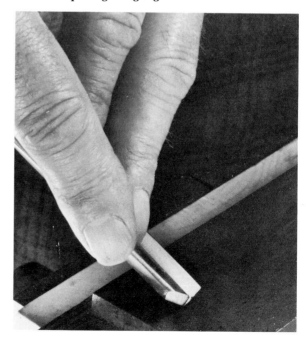

C:2. Finishing the gouge.

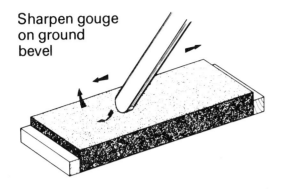

Sharpen gouge
on ground
bevel

C:3. Rock the gouge as you run it along the stone.

The final finish can be given to the gouge by rotating it while holding it at right angles to the stone, and moving it lengthways along the stone. Some users will care to use a leather strop dressed with a mixture of flour and emery powder or some other cutting compound. This strop rubbed several times along the bevel will produce a very high-quality finish. Alternatively, you can use the rubberized abrasive stick, which is flexible rubber impregnated with silicon-carbide cutting grit. These sticks can be used dry and they produce a perfect surface without additions.

The chisel should have both bevels ground at a 30° included angle and again be sharpened on the ground face, as should the parting tool. Place the ground bevel on the stone and move it backwards and forwards along the stone, preferably in a figure-8 movement to distribute wear over the entire surface of the stone. Do this on both bevels until a burr appears and finally breaks away; then the tool should be ready for use. Once again, the bevel can be further improved by stropping on the leather strop or by using a rubberized abrasive stick.

Sharpen on both ground
bevels, keep the bevels
flat

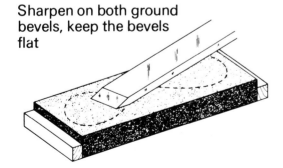

C:4. Sharpening the chisel.

A group of woodturning tools which we must not ignore are the scraper-type chisels. These tools require careful sharpening, but they are applied in a different way to the wood. They should be ground at 10° on one side only and be sharpened on this face. The tools are first burnished with a ticketer made from a piece of hard, round steel, or a small three-quarter file with the teeth ground away and the corners rolled over. The edge is then turned over to form a tiny hook which actually does the cutting.

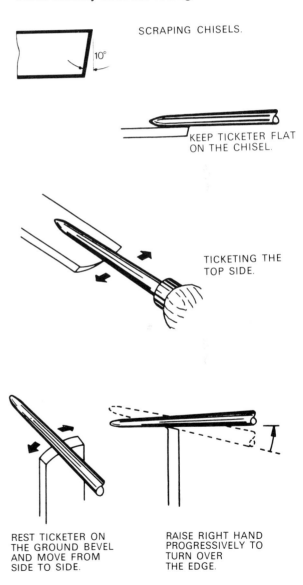

SCRAPING CHISELS.

10°

KEEP TICKETER FLAT
ON THE CHISEL.

TICKETING THE
TOP SIDE.

REST TICKETER ON
THE GROUND BEVEL
AND MOVE FROM
SIDE TO SIDE.

RAISE RIGHT HAND
PROGRESSIVELY TO
TURN OVER
THE EDGE.

C:5-6. Sharpening the scraping chisels.

Appendix D

Using the Tools

There are very few rules to learn, but certain precautions must be taken at the outset.

- The wood must be firmly held.
- The tool rest must be placed in the correct position.
- Not only must the tools be correctly ground, but they must be sharpened on the ground bevel. Great attention must be paid to the fine quality of the edge, since it all starts there.

Cutting between centers, or spindle turning

Fix the tool rest slightly above center height. Place either the shallow or the deep-fluted gouge on the rest, left hand well up to the cutting edge, right hand down at the extremity of the handle. The bevel should be facing the wood so that when the right hand raises the gouge, the bevel will run on the wood. By raising the right hand farther, the cutting edge will come into contact with the revolving wood and begin cutting. The tool is sloped in the direction of movement along the tee rest, and the center of the gouge will do the cutting.

Cutting can be carried out by moving either toward or away from the headstock. For very heavy cutting, use a long and strong gouge, the handle of which can rest against the body for additional support. The bevel of the tools will rub the wood after the point of cut; it follows, therefore, that the better the finish on the bevel, the better will be the burnished finish of the wood.

After using the gouge, a perfect surface can be arrived at only with the chisel. Use either the skew chisel or one ground square across. The rule is exactly as stated previously: place the chisel on the tool rest, let its bevel rub on the wood and raise the right hand to bring on the cut. The thickness of the cut will depend on the amount the hand is raised. Slope the chisel in the direction of the movement; the center of the chisel will do the cutting and the bevel will burnish the wood after the point of cut. A perfect surface will result and it will be done in complete safety with this two-point method of tool support.

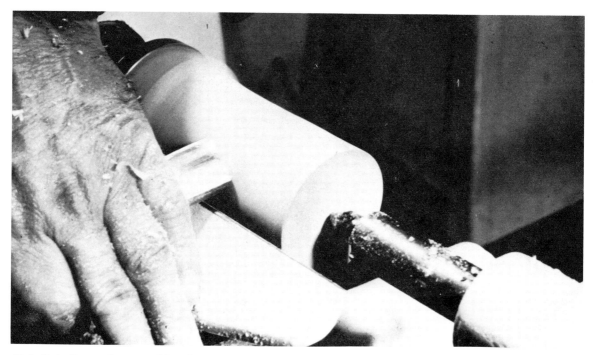

D:1. Spindle turning–roughing down to size.

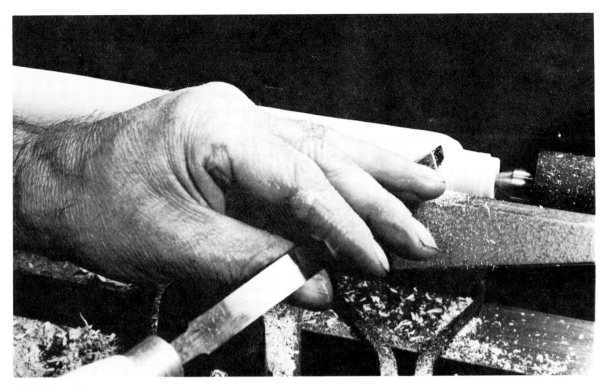

D:2. Rounding over.

D:3. Squaring ends and shoulders.

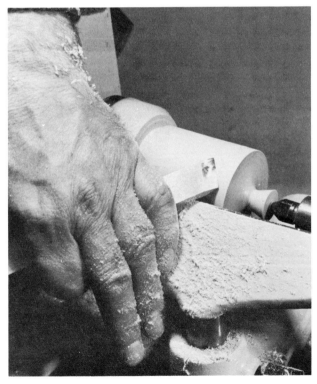

D:4. The chisel can be used for beading.

D:5. Tapering.

Bowl Work

The *deep flute gouge*, preferably ⅜ in (9.6 mm) in size, is the ideal tool for bowl work. The rule is the same as for spindle work: the bevel "looks at" and rubs the work, and the cut is brought on by the movement of the right hand. Once again, the center or slightly below the center of the tool does the work. When cutting the outside, the bevel follows the curve.

Cutting the inside starts from a small groove or starting point. With the bevel rub-

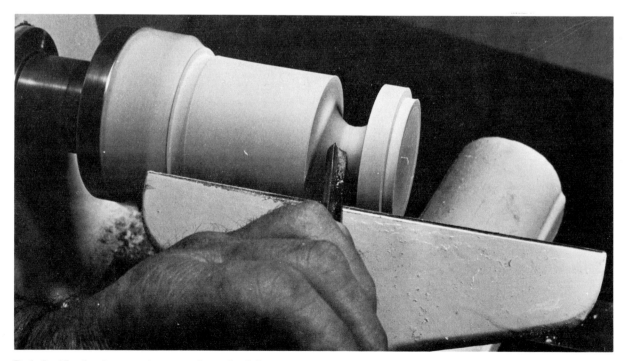

D:6. Inside shaping—cutting cove from the left.

D:7. Inside shaping—cutting cove from the right.

D:8. Boring the center with the roundnose gouge.

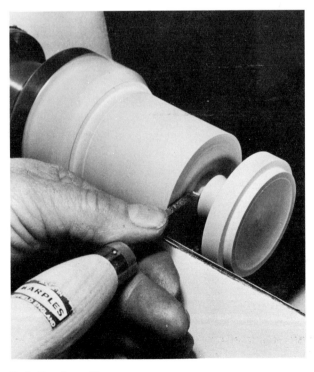

D:9. Parting off.

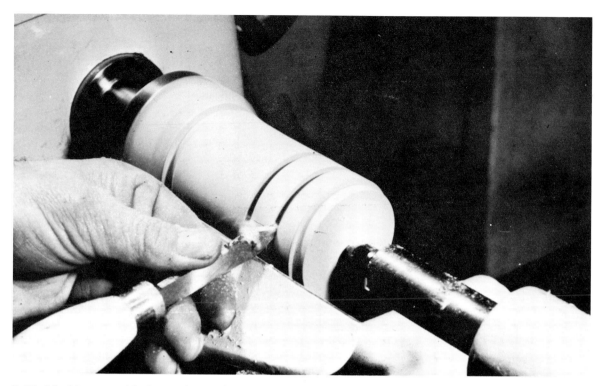

D:10. Marking out with the parting tool.

bing, the right hand is raised to bring on the cut. At the same time, as the tool moves toward the center of the bowl, the tool itself is brought up so that the center of the tool meets the center of the bowl, with the depth of cut exactly maintained.

Index

auger, 174

between-centers holding,
    176-177
bowl gouge, 174
bowl work, 186-187
bread dish with handle, 37-38
breakfast, projects for,
    164-171
bud vase, 11-14
butter dish, 105-107

candleholder, 6-10
carafe, 64-67
carving board, 74-75
cheese board, 98-100
Child coil chuck, 179
coasters, 17
coffee grinder, 149-156
coffee (Seventh Course),
    projects for, 126-135
collar chuck, 179, 181
collet chuck, 179, 180
counterboring tool, 177
cracker and butter dish,
    101-104
cracker barrel, 108-111
cup chuck, 178
cups and saucers, 126-132

dairy (Fifth Course), projects
    for, 98-111
dessert (Fourth Course),
    projects for, 92-97
dinner mats, 15-17
dinner plates and side plates,
    47-51
driving fork, 176

egg cups, 168-171

faceplate, 178
flatbit, 175
fruit bowl, 92-95
fruit dish, 96-97

goblet, 59-63
gouges, 172
    sharpening, 182-183
grapefruit dish, 28-33

holding wood for turning,
    176-181
hors d'oeuvre dish, 24-27

kitchen, projects for, 140-163

lathe headstock holding,
    178-181

laying the table, projects for, 6-23
lip and spur drill, 175

main dish (Third Course), projects for, 47-91
mandrel, 177
marmalade (or jam) pot top, 164-167
mortar and pestle, 142-143
mustard pot, 72-73

napkin rings, 18-23
nut bowl with waste rim, 112-116
nut bowl with wheel cracker, 122-125
nut dish with pick container, 117-121
nutmeg grinder, 144-148
nuts (Sixth Course), projects for, 112-125

parting tool, 173
pepper mill, 42-43
petit fours dish, 136-139
petit fours (Eighth Course), projects for, 136-139
pin mandrel, 180, 181
potato masher, 159-163

rolling pin, 157-158

salad servers, 68-71
salt and pepper shakers, 44-46
salt mill, 81-88
sauce-bottle holder with lid, 76-80
sawtooth cutter, 175
scraping chisel, 174
    sharpening, 183
screw chuck, 178
sharpening the tools, 182-183
side salad dishes, 52-58
six-in-one chuck, 179, 180
    as screw chuck, 181
sizing tool, 173
skew chisel, 173
soup bowl, 34-36
soup (Second Course), projects for, 34-36
spindle gouges, 172
spindle turning, 184-186
split ring, 180, 181
starters (First Course), projects for, 24-33
steak tenderizer, 140-141
sugar bowl, 133-135

toast rack, 39-41
tools, 172-175

wine bottle, 89-91
wood drill, 175

Acknowledgments

The thanks of the author to the following:

Record Ridgway Tools Ltd., for use of halftones; also Coronet Tool Co. Ltd., Derby, and Woodcraft Supply (U.K.) Ltd.

To Elspeth Flowerday for typing the manuscript.

To my wife for her patience and acceptance of neglect when writing, photography and drawing took preference.

To Charles Nurnberg for his encouragement, and the staff of Sterling Publishing Co., Inc., for all their help.